WESTMORELAND COUNTY
PENNSYLVANIA

1783 CENSUS

REPRINTED FROM
Pennsylvania Archives

HERITAGE BOOKS
2011

HERITAGE BOOKS
AN IMPRINT OF HERITAGE BOOKS, INC.

Books, CDs, and more—Worldwide

For our listing of thousands of titles see our website
at
www.HeritageBooks.com

Published 2011 by
HERITAGE BOOKS, INC.
Publishing Division
100 Railroad Ave. #104
Westminster, Maryland 21157

Published by Family Line Publications 1990

All rights reserved. No part of this book may be reproduced or transmitted in any form or by any means, electronic or mechanical, including photocopying, recording or by any information storage and retrieval system without written permission from the author, except for the inclusion of brief quotations in a review.

International Standard Book Numbers
Paperbound: 978-1-58549-173-5
Clothbound: 978-0-7884-8842-9

CONTENTS

Rostraver Township 1
Franklyn Township 10
Tyrone Township 16
Derry Township 20
Pitt Township 23
Hempfield Township 26
Huntington Township 31
Springhill Township 40
Mount Pleasant Township 49
Armstrong Township 56
Fairfield Township 58
Donnegal Township 59
Manallen Township 60
Index 65

Compiler Note

This listing as taken exactly as written in the published
Third Series of Pennsylvania Acrhives. The spelling of
names has not been changed.

WESTMORELAND COUNTY RETURN of 1783

Rostraver Township

	Acres	Horses	Cattle	Sheep	Inhabitants White	Black
Allen, David	--	2	2	3	5	--
Allen, Benja'n	--	4	2	3	5	--
Andrews, Will'm,	200	3	3	6	8	--
Alben, Will'm	150	2	3	5	8	--
Armstrong, Tho's,	--	2	2	--	4	--
Alexander, Adam	--	2	2	--	7	--
Archer, Joseph	--	1	2	--	3	--
Applegate, Dan'l	275	4	6	4	10	--
Applegate, Sam'l	--	1	2	2	6	--
Applegate, Benj'n	300	2	4	10	6	--
Anderson, Will'm	--	1	1	--	3	--
Allen, Will'm	--	1	1	--	5	--
Applegate, Will'm	300	3	5	8	11	--
Adair, Will'm, single	--	--	--	--	1	--
Blakeley, Rob't	300	3	3	6	5	--
Burns, Sam'l	300	--	--	--	--	--
Baker, And'w	100	2	1	--	7	--
Burgess, Ann	70	1	1	--	7	2
Brownlow, James	--	3	4	--	7	--
Becket, Mary	400	2	4	5	3	--
Burgan, Dan'l	--	2	1	4	6	--
Baxter, Sam'l	--	2	2	--	10	--
Bovel, John	50	1	4	6	8	--
Briggs, John	--	2	1	--	3	--
Barrackman, George	100	2	3	2	5	--
Barrackhamer, John	70	2	3	4	7	--
Burch, John	--	1	1	--	8	--
Burges, Richard, single	--	1	--	--	1	--
Brownlow, Thomas	--	--	--	--	1	--
Burcham, Benijah	50	2	1	3	8	--
Bowman, Jacob	--	1	1	--	8	--
Brown, Benj'n	30	--	--	--	1	--
Burns, Arthur	200	2	4	--	8	--
Barrackman, Mich'l	--	--	1	--	6	--
Broddy, Will'm	--	3	2	7	8	--
Barrackman, Peter	500	4	6	7	8	1
Berger, Fred'k	--	1	--	--	7	--
Boyd, Nath'l	250	2	3	8	6	--
Boyd, Widow	--	--	1	--	1	--
Biggart, Sam'l	150	3	2	3	7	--
Barns, Robert	--	2	2	--	7	--
Budd, Joseph	430	3	3	2	3	--
Bedsworth, Joseph	150	2	3	3	5	--
Becket, Joseph	300	2	4	6	5	2
Broddy, Hugh	150	2	3	5	5	--
Brant, Barney	--	1	2	4	6	--
Budd, Joshua	150	2	3	2	4	--
Becket, John	--	2	2	--	7	--
Barkley, John	--	1	1	--	4	--
Bazel, Mathew	200	2	3	5	10	--
Boner, Mathew	200	2	2	--	4	--

Rostraver Township	Acres	Horses	Cattle	Sheep	White	Black
Biggart, John, single	--	--	--	--	1	--
Brant, Edw'd, d'o	--	--	--	--	1	--
Barkley, Joseph, d'o	--	--	--	--	1	--
Bazel, Math'w, Jun'r, d'o	--	--	--	--	1	--
Copstick, Sam'l	--	1	1	--	3	--
Caldwell, Rob't	--	1	1	--	10	--
Clark, George	300	--	1	4	3	--
Clark, Sam'l	--	2	2	--	6	--
Casselman, Will'm	--	2	1	2	6	--
Craig, John	--	2	2	--	9	--
Clemmons, John	275	1	4	7	2	--
Chamberlain, Tho's	--	2	2	2	4	--
Casselman, John	--	2	4	6	8	--
Clemmons, Sam'l	300	2	1	1	7	--
Clark, Benj'n, single	--	1	1	--	3	--
Calvin, Will'm	--	1	1	--	10	--
Cunningham, Will'm, single	60	1	--	--	1	--
Cook, Edw'd, Esq'r	1,500	5	10	15	7	6
Cockeyowens, John	300	--	--	--	--	--
Clemons, Ferguson	--	1	2	--	5	--
Cort, Joseph	--	2	4	4	9	--
Camp, Joseph	--	1	1	--	2	--
Case, Butler, Sen'r	--	2	3	2	6	--
Clark, Nath'l	--	1	1	--	6	--
Clark, Benj'n, Sen'r	--	--	2	1	6	--
Chambers, Edward	3	2	3	4	8	--
Casselman, Henry, single	--	--	--	--	1	--
Cheney, Will'm, d'o	--	--	--	--	1	--
Crawford, George	200	--	--	--	--	--
Chambers, John	--	1	1	--	4	--
Case, Meshach	--	2	1	2	3	--
Cue, James	50	2	2	--	--	--
Calhoon, Adley	300	2	4	3	5	--
Craighead, Rob't	400	3	4	10	9	--
Cuppage, Isaac	--	1	2	--	6	4
Cavett, John	150	2	4	3	8	--
Craig, Alexander	200	2	2	--	7	--
Carmical, Daniel, single	--	2	1	--	2	--
Carmical, John, d'o	--	--	--	--	1	--
Case, Butler, d'o	--	--	--	--	1	--
Calhoon, Thomas	--	2	2	4	4	--
Carroll, Taylor	--	--	2	--	3	--
Campbell, Henry	--	2	2	3	3	--
Dungan, Nathan	--	2	1	1	3	--
Dunn, Will'm	250	2	4	4	8	--
Dixon, Silas	80	--	--	--	--	--
Drum, Philip	--	1	1	--	7	--
Darr, Mich'l	--	2	2	2	4	--
Dehaven, Isaac	--	1	1	--	8	--
Decker, Jacob	--	1	2	--	5	--
Dungan, John, single	--	1	--	--	1	--
Dungan, Joseph	--	--	--	--	1	--
Drennon, John	300	2	2	6	5	--
Drenon, Will'm	--	1	2	--	4	--
Davidson, Will'm	--	2	1	6	5	--

Rostraver Township	Acres	Horses	Cattle	Sheep	White/Black
Dousman, John	100	--	--	--	--	--
Duff, Oliver	--	2	6	3	8	--
Duff, Alexander	--	2	2	2	8	--
Duff, John	--	2	2	--	2	--
Davis, Benjamin	550	3	4	10	6	4
Davis, Azariah	350	--	--	--	1	--
Devore, Moses	50	2	--	--	2	--
Dye, John	300	1	2	2	4	--
Devore, Sam'l	300	2	2	--	4	2
Drenon, Thomas, single	--	1	--	--	1	--
Downey, Will'm, d'o	--	--	--	--	1	--
Dougharty, -----	--	1	--	--	2	--
Elrod, Tedor	150	3	2	3	7	--
Elliot, John, single	300	1	--	--	1	--
Ekin, Alex'r	--	--	2	--	--	7
Ekin, James, single	--	2	2	--	1	--
Ekin, Rob't	--	2	2	4	9	--
Evans, Edw'd, single	--	1	--	--	1	--
Emley, John	100	2	2	7	5	--
Earl, Rob't	113	1	2	--	6	--
Fell, Benjamin	380	3	8	9	10	--
Finley, Ja's, Rev'd	300	--	--	--	--	--
Fryar, Rob't	--	1	1	--	6	--
Forsythe, Will'm	200	2	3	5	11	--
Forsythe, Rob't, single	200	1	1	2	2	--
Fulton, Sam'l	--	2	2	2	6	--
Flemming, John	--	2	--	--	4	--
Fleck, John, Sen'r	100	2	3	3	8	--
Frost, James	--	2	3	3	6	--
Fell, John	--	1	--	--	2	--
Finney, James, Jun'r	300	2	3	--	8	--
Fleck, John Ju'r, single	--	1	--	--	1	--
Finley, David	--	--	--	--	--	--
Finney, James	150	4	4	6	5	--
Finney, Ja's and Rob't Smith	270	--	--	--	--	--
Finney, Will'm	150	2	3	1	3	--
Fockler, Adam	200	--	--	--	--	--
Foster, Benjamin, single	--	--	--	--	1	--
Finley, John	--	2	3	6	5	--
Fitch, John, single	200	2	1	--	2	--
Garr, Gasper	250	2	3	6	9	1
Gardner, Will'm, Sen'r	300	1	1	--	6	1
Gardner, Will'm	--	1	1	--	3	--
Goe, William	750	8	8	17	13	9
Greer, Lawrence	--	1	1	--	3	--
Gorby, Thomas	100	2	2	1	8	--
Gaston, Alexander	--	2	--	--	5	--
Greer, James	--	2	3	5	4	--
Goudy, John	--	2	2	--	8	--
Grist, William	--	2	1	--	4	--
Green, Tamor	--	--	--	--	4	1
Glass, Robert, single	--	1	--	--	1	--
Goe, John, d'o	--	--	--	--	--	--
Gardner, Will'm, Jun'r	300	1	1	--	4	--
Gardner, Arch'd, single	--	--	--	--	1	--

Rostraver Township	Acres	Horses	Cattle	Sheep	White	Black
Greer, Isaac	150	2	2	--	5	--
Greer, John	100	2	3	8	6	--
Gray, Robert	300	2	2	--	4	--
Gordon, Arch'd, single	--	3	1	--	1	--
Glenn, Will'm	--	2	1	--	6	--
Gibb, Hugh, single	--	2	2	2	7	--
Gaston, John	300	--	4	2	10	--
Gaston, William, single	--	1	2	4	3	--
Gilmore, John, d'o	150	2	3	6	3	--
Gilmore, David, single	150	--	--	--	1	--
Gratz, Barnard	250	--	--	--	--	--
Gilmore, William, single	--	--	--	--	1	--
Hudskins, Sam'l, single	--	1	--	--	1	--
Hill, Joseph, Sen'r	300	5	4	8	2	5
Hill, Step'n	--	--	2	--	3	--
Hill, Joseph, Jun	200	2	4	5	6	1
Harris, Benj'n	450	1	2	6	5	--
Holmes, Sam'l	--	2	3	4	7	--
Hutten, Mary	300	4	7	11	1	12
Hughes, John, single	--	1	--	--	1	3
Hynes, Alex'r	130	2	3	5	6	--
Housman, Chris'r	150	2	5	6	9	--
Housman, John	50	1	1	1	7	--
Hoover, Peter	95	3	2	4	8	--
Hammond, Dan'l	300	4	6	15	5	--
Heldibrant, Philip	--	2	2	5	9	--
Hammond, James	150	--	--	--	--	--
Hammond, Sam'l, single	--	--	--	1	--	
Howel, Luellen	300	3	8	4	6	--
Howel, Philip, single	--	1	--	--	--	1
Harra, Charles	370	4	4	12	11	1
Hamilton, James, single	--	2	--	--	1	--
Humes, John, d'o	--	1	--	--	1	--
Hall, Joseph	150	2	2	--	5	--
Hall, Step'n	150	2	2	--	6	--
Hall, Henry	--	2	3	3	2	--
Hart, Elizah	70	1	2	--	3	--
Hogg, Mich'l	300	1	2	2	6	1
Headen, Chris'r	--	1	1	4	4	--
Hall, Will'm	60	2	3	2	3	--
Hersha, Peter, single	300	1	--	--	1	--
Hall, John, d'o	--	--	--	--	1	--
Howel, Andrew, d'o	--	--	--	--	1	--
Jamison, Rob't	75	2	3	1	6	--
Jamison, Math'w	75	1	--	--	1	--
Jones, Edward	--	1	1	--	5	--
Johnson, Andrew	200	--	--	--	--	--
Ingle, John	--	2	2	3	5	--
Johnson, Richard	200	3	6	6	6	1
Johnson, James, single	--	2	2	2	5	--
Johnson, Peter	100	1	2	--	2	--
Jones, Thomas	--	2	3	4	4	--
Jones, Joseph, Sen.	--	3	5	9	7	3
Jones, William, single	80	1	--	--	1	--
Johnson, Jonathan	300	3	5	5	8	4

Rostraver Township	Acres	Horses	Cattle	Sheep	White	Black
Jones, Jacob	--	2	2	5	5	--
Kirk, Vincent	--	--	1	--	3	--
Keller, Peter	50	--	1	--	5	--
Kerr, Rob't	--	1	1	--	4	--
Kelly, James	--	2	3	--	5	--
Kerns, John	300	--	--	--	--	--
Kepley, Chris'r	--	2	1	--	10	--
Kelly, John	300	2	3	4	8	--
Kennedy, Rob't	100	1	1	--	2	--
Kennedy, Will'm, Sen'r	100	--	1	--	2	--
Kennedy, Hugh	100	--	--	--	--	--
Kennedy, Will'm, Jun'r	100	1	2	2	7	--
Kerr, Will'm	--	2	2	6	6	--
Kerr, Joseph, single	--	2	1	--	2	--
Kerroll, Joseph	150	3	4	--	5	--
Kent, Thomas	--	2	2	2	5	--
Ketchem, Steph'n	1700	2	3	8	4	--
Ketchem, Will'm	164	3	6	6	6	--
Kyle, John	400	3	4	10	10	--
Kilgore, John, single	--	--	--	--	1	--
Lindsey, Will'm	350	2	7	6	4	1
Lerue, Abra'm	150	2	1	--	3	--
Lowry, Steph'n	300	3	--	--	2	1
Linn, And'w, Jun'r	300	--	--	--	--	--
Long, Benj'n	--	1	3	2	5	--
Long, Thomas	--	1	4	5	8	--
Little, Samuel	--	--	1	--	3	--
Lowry, John, single	--	--	--	--	1	--
Littleton, John, d'o	--	--	--	--	1	--
Logan, John, single	--	1	--	--	1	--
Lock, Benjamin	--	--	1	--	7	--
Lemon, Henry	100	2	2	4	4	--
Lowry, Steph'n	--	1	2	--	5	--
Lowry, James	--	1	2	--	7	--
Lemon, Joseph	150	1	1	--	6	--
Linn, John	--	2	2	4	6	--
Lappin, William	--	1	1	--	8	--
Larrimore, Sam'l, single	--	--	--	--	1	--
Lemon, Thomas	--	1	2	--	3	--
Landers, John	--	1	2	--	3	--
Lanterman, Peter	--	2	1	--	--	--
Lattimore, George	200	--	--	--	--	--
McClure, George	150	2	--	--	2	--
Morgan, Morgan	250	1	2	4	2	--
Moreland, Jason	100	2	3	6	9	--
Mullen, James	--	1	2	--	7	--
Morehead, Joseph	30	1	1	2	6	--
McKee, Will'm	--	2	4	--	8	--
Morehead, Alex'r	250	3	5	2	11	--
Morelin, Rich'd, single	200	3	4	8	5	--
McIntire, John	--	--	1	--	3	--
McIntire, Will'm	--	1	1	--	4	--
McGaughan, Mark	--	1	2	2	4	--
McGruder, Hezekiah	259	4	--	--	13	--
Mills, Edward	--	1	1	--	2	--

Rostraver Township	Acres	Horses	Cattle	Sheep	White	Black
McGinnis, Tho's	--	3	3	5	6	--
Mitchell, Hannah	100	2	2	3	3	--
McGarraugh, Jos., Esq'r	300	3	3	4	8	--
McCune, And'w	--	1	1	--	5	--
McLaughlin, Edw'd	--	1	2	--	5	--
Moore, Rob't	--	2	2	10	4	--
Moorehead, Tho's	700	3	3	4	6	--
Morgan, Will'm	200	2	3	2	7	--
McCune, Thomas	--	3	4	2	11	--
Mackey, William	--	1	--	--	1	1
Maxwell, James	--	1	--	--	4	--
Martin, Geo Adam	150	1	2	4	4	--
Mastin, Peter	--	3	4	--	8	--
Martin, Joshua, single	--	--	--	--	1	--
Milburn, David, d'o	--	--	--	--	--	--
Mitchell, Edw'd	40	--	1	2	2	--
McRight, Will'm, single	115	1	--	--	1	--
McLean, Joseph	100	3	4	6	1	--
Maxwell, John	--	2	1	3	4	--
Mitchell, Math'w	150	2	2	4	8	--
McConnell, Adam, single	170	1	--	--	1	--
McConnell, Adam, Sen'r	--	2	2	3	5	--
McConnell, John, single	100	1	--	--	1	--
Moore, Will'm	300	3	3	10	6	--
Morton, Thomas	150	2	3	3	3	--
Morton, William	--	1	--	--	3	--
Muse, Fantley	--	2	2	--	3	--
McClure, James	--	1	1	2	7	--
McKinney, Math'w	300	3	3	3	6	--
Mitchel, Sam'l	--	2	1	3	7	--
Moore, James, Sen'r	200	--	--	--	--	--
Moore, James	200	2	2	4	7	--
McMeans, Rob't	50	1	2	--	6	--
McNeal, John	--	2	2	2	3	--
Matthew, James	--	2	3	4	7	--
Mitchell, Ebenezer	150	2	2	3	6	--
Mitchell, Will'm	--	2	5	4	6	--
Mitchell, John	300	4	5	6	5	--
Mitchell, Joseph	--	2	2	--	4	--
Mitchell, John, Sen'r	--	2	2	--	7	--
McLaughlin, Sam'l	--	3	3	2	5	--
Mooney, James	--	1	1	2	2	--
McLain, Abijah	--	2	2	5	4	--
McLain, Rob't	285	3	2	4	8	--
Mappins, James	--	1	4	4	7	--
McKnight, Tho's	200	2	2	--	4	--
Moore, Forgy	--	1	2	--	4	--
Mitchel, Alex'r	150	2	3	4	6	--
Magnor, Redman	200	2	3	2	5	--
McElroy, Will'm	200	2	2	2	10	--
Montgomery, Hugh	--	1	1	--	7	--
Mitchell, Robert, single	--	--	--	--	1	--
Mitchell, Rob't	--	1	2	--	--	--
McKinney, Henry, single	--	--	--	--	1	--
McLaughlin, Henry, d'o	--	--	--	--	1	--

Rostraver Township	Acres	Horses	Cattle	Sheep	White	Black
McConnell, Rob't	300	2	5	5	11	--
Murphy, Hugh	--	2	1	--	--	--
McCarty, Rob't	--	1	--	--	1	--
McCoy, Sam'l	300	--	--	--	--	--
Nipley, Mary	250	2	1	2	8	--
Neesbit, John	--	2	2	4	3	--
Nigh, Jacob	--	1	2	--	7	--
Newel, Sam'l	--	2	2	6	10	--
Nornival, John	--	2	1	2	4	--
Nitterfield, W'm, single	--	1	--	--	1	--
Nash, Thomas	--	2	2	2	5	--
Oldham, Isaac	--	2	3	2	7	--
Ogden, David	--	1	1	--	3	--
Owens, Thomas, single	--	--	--	--	--	--
Patterson, Peter	130	2	3	6	6	--
Patterson, Thomas, single	150	1	1	--	1	--
Patterson, John, single	150	1	--	--	1	--
Patterson, John, smith	300	3	3	3	7	--
Pressor, Henry	--	3	2	8	7	--
Patton, Joseph	300	1	1	2	6	--
Paul, Jacob	--	1	2	--	5	--
Pitts, Will'm	100	3	3	--	5	2
Powers, James, Rev'd	300	--	--	--	--	--
Pierce, Lewis	485	3	4	4	8	--
Pierce, Joseph, Jun'r, single	285	--	--	--	1	--
Pierce, John	400	3	6	4	7	--
Purdy, Rob't	100	2	--	--	5	--
Patterson, Rob't	--	3	3	--	7	--
Patterson, James, single	150	1	--	--	1	--
Pierce, Charles	40	2	2	3	5	--
Pritchard, Rich'd	--	2	2	--	2	--
Pierce, And'w, Sen'r	200	4	4	8	6	--
Pettit, Jerem'h	--	1	1	--	10	--
Perry, James	300	2	5	--	6	2
Pierce, James	200	3	3	6	4	--
Pierce, And'w	200	4	3	8	8	1
Points, Nath'l, single	--	1	--	--	1	--
Pierce, Joseph, Sen'r	500	2	4	7	14	--
Quillen, Ambrose	--	1	1	--	3	--
Rammage, Will'm, single	--	1	--	--	1	--
Ryan, John	200	2	4	4	8	2
Reed, John	--	2	5	2	10	--
Ryan, Mich'l	--	2	2	1	6	--
Robison, Alex'r	300	4	5	7	10	--
Ritchey, Will'm	--	--	1	--	4	--
Reeves, Abner	100	2	4	3	--	--
Ritchy, Abr'm	--	2	1	3	8	--
Rattan, John	160	2	3	4	5	--
Ritchy, Will'm, sen'r	200	3	4	3	4	--
Resnor, Peter	300	4	8	10	7	4
Rogers, And'w	--	1	2	--	6	--
Robb, Nich's	--	2	2	--	7	--
Rankin, Wm.	200	3	3	8	7	--
Robb, Isaac	--	1	1	--	3	--
Ritchy, Will'm	300	2	2	4	5	--

Rostraver Township	Acres	Horses	Cattle	Sheep	White	Black
Robison, David	300	4	3	9	6	--
Rardon, John	50	2	2	1	5	2
Ralston, Joseph	--	1	3	3	3	--
Robison, And'w	200	6	5	4	4	--
Robins, Obed'h	--	1	2	1	6	--
Reed, James, single	--	--	--	--	1	--
Steward, James	50	2	3	6	5	--
Stevens, Thomas	--	2	--	--	3	--
Syphritz, Joseph	--	2	1	3	10	--
Stivers, Rubin	--	1	1	--	4	--
Sterret, James	--	2	2	--	4	--
Shephard, Henry	--	2	1	--	3	--
Shaver, Paul	--	3	3	5	5	--
Shaver, Jacob	--	1	1	1	4	--
Sheppard, Solomon	--	1	3	--	11	--
Springer, Mich'l	330	3	6	10	5	--
Speers, Rogana	250	6	5	10	5	9
Sands, James	--	2	2	--	10	--
Steward, John	100	2	4	3	3	--
Scott, John	--	1	2	--	6	--
Stoolfire, Chris'r	--	--	2	2	6	--
Shipler, Peter	150	3	3	8	10	--
Shipler, Mathias	150	3	5	8	7	--
Shipler, Philip	150	3	5	5	5	--
Swearingen, Van	400	--	--	--	--	--
Sinnet, Jacob	--	1	--	--	4	--
Stevens, John, Sen'r	--	3	2	3	4	--
Stevens, John, Jun'r	--	1	1	1	3	--
Sweany, Thomas	--	2	3	--	7	--
Stevens, Levy	800	3	3	8	4	1
Staret, Joseph, single	--	1	--	--	1	--
Sunderlin, John, single	--	1	--	--	1	--
Syphred, Jacob, d'o	--	--	--	--	1	--
Shaver, Will'm, d'o	--	--	--	--	1	--
Springer, Mich'l, Jun'r, single	--	--	--	--	1	--
Springer, John, d'o	--	--	--	--	1	--
Spears, Jacob	--	--	--	--	1	--
Swards, Sam'l	100	--	--	--	2	--
Shaver, John, single	--	--	--	--	1	--
Shields, George	115	2	3	--	7	--
Steward, John	300	1	2	--	--	--
Smith, Will'm	--	2	3	2	4	--
Simpson, Joseph	--	--	3	1	7	--
St. Clair, Gen'l	240	5	4	--	7	1
Sill, Will'm	--	1	--	--	1	--
Sill, George	100	2	3	4	10	--
Standiford, Eph'm	--	2	1	2	11	--
Sampson, John	250	--	3	6	7	--
Steward, Thomas	--	--	1	--	9	--
Steel, Joseph	--	3	3	5	8	--
Steel, James	--	1	--	--	1	--
Steward, James	150	3	4	6	9	--
Steel, Will'm	--	2	2	2	3	--
Sutton, David	--	2	--	--	5	--
Sampson, Will'm, single	150	1	2	--	2	--

Rostraver Township	Acres	Horses	Cattle	Sheep	White/Black
Scott, James	--	2	2	3	4	--
Shelah, Mich'l	--	2	2	--	2	--
Sparks, Benj'n	200	2	2	2	4	--
Sparks, Richard	170	2	4	8	4	--
Sparks, Walter	150	1	1	3	4	--
Summerville, John	300	4	5	--	7	--
Sampson, Tho's, single	--	--	--	--	1	--
Stinson, James, d'o	--	--	--	--	1	--
Stevens, Isaac	--	2	--	--	1	--
Scott, Sam'l	250	2	3	3	6	--
Swearingen, Van	300	--	--	--	--	--
Teagarden, Dan'l	--	1	1	--	2	--
Thompson, Moses	100	2	4	7	7	--
Thompson, John, single	20	2	1	--	5	--
Thorn, Robert	--	4	3	2	9	--
Tully, Aaron	50	2	3	1	5	--
Thompson, James	--	1	1	1	2	--
Tanner, Philip	300	--	--	--	--	--
Taylor, George	--	2	2	--	2	--
Taylor, Henry, single	--	--	--	--	--	--
Thorn, Joseph	--	2	2	5	7	--
Taylor, Isaac, single	--	2	--	--	1	--
Thompson, Dan'l	200	3	3	6	3	--
Thompson, Cornel's, single	300	3	5	5	2	--
Thompson, Dan'l	200	3	3	6	3	--
Vanmeter, John	300	4	7	15	9	--
Voucher, Peter	--	3	1	8	6	--
Vandolan, Peter	200	3	3	3	8	--
Vantrese, Isaac	110	2	3	2	4	--
Vanmeter, Jacob	600	3	3	3	8	--
Vance, William	--	1	1	2	6	--
Walker, Ebenezer	300	2	--	8	7	--
Worley, John	--	2	2	2	4	--
Wiseman, John	400	2	4	7	7	1
Wickerham, Adam	150	--	--	--	--	--
Walker, James	--	2	2	5	5	--
Warman, Joseph	--	2	2	4	9	--
Walker, Rob't	--	1	1	--	5	--
Walker, Will'm	--	2	2	3	4	--
Warren, Thomas	--	3	3	7	7	4
Warnock, Will'm	--	1	3	--	11	--
Wright, John	300	2	4	1	8	1
Willson, Sam'l	250	1	5	5	8	--
White, And'w	40	2	1	--	6	--
Wrothwell, Peter	200	1	1	--	4	--
Westbay, Henry	200	5	5	4	9	--
Walker, Rob't	--	--	2	2	4	--
Wilson, Rob't	--	2	2	3	6	--
Whitaker, John	100	2	3	--	10	--
Withrow, Will'm	300	3	4	3	4	--
Wilson, Hugh & Tho's, single	200	2	3	1	4	--
Wilson, James	250	4	3	--	6	--
Wilson, Joseph	150	1	2	--	4	--
Waddle, Peter	500	2	3	2	4	--
Wilson, Will'm	--	2	2	3	7	--

Rostraver Township	Acres	Horses	Cattle	Sheep	White	/Black
Wall, Walter	300	3	7	12	8	--
Williams, David	300	3	2	--	10	--
Williams, James	--	1	1	2	2	--
Wall, James	300	3	8	10	8	--
Wilson, Zach's	150	2	2	--	4	--
Walker, John	--	2	1	1	2	--
Wilson, Isaac	150	3	3	5	9	--
Wilson, Aaron	150	3	5	7	6	--
Waddle, James	150	1	1	--	2	--
Waddle, Dan'l	150	2	2	2	4	--
Waddle, John	--	2	4	--	10	2
Warner, Joseph	200	3	5	8	7	--
Walling, Thomas	200	2	2	--	4	--
Wilson, Adam, single	--	1	--	--	1	--
Woolsey, Will'm	300	--	--	--	--	--
Total inhabitants	--	--	--	--	2,350	107

Franklyn Township

	Acres	Horses	Cattle	Sheep	Inhabitants White	Black
Allen, John	--	2	--	--	6	--
Alexander, Mary	80	1	1	--	4	--
Adams, James	--	4	5	6	4	--
Archibald, Benj'n	--	1	3	1	12	--
Arnold, And'w	350	3	5	8	10	--
Allen, David	200	3	4	3	4	--
Allen, John, Esq'r	160	2	3	6	7	--
Allen, James, single	150	1	1	--	1	--
Burns, Sam'l	300	3	5	5	8	--
Burns, Patrick	--	3	3	3	8	--
Baul, Richard	--	3	2	10	7	--
Boyars, Sam'l	--	1	--	--	2	--
Boys, James	390	2	6	12	9	--
Bradford, Widow	--	3	7	15	4	--
Bradley, Moses	--	--	--	--	4	--
Barker, Will'm	150	6	4	--	5	--
Barker, Joseph	60	2	2	6	5	--
Barkley, Elijah	125	2	2	3	5	--
Brown, Eliezer	100	1	1	--	6	--
Brown, Nathan	200	2	2	4	4	--
Becket, Joseph	200	1	2	6	6	--
Boyers, Sam'l	--	2	2	6	10	--
Boyers, James	150	2	2	2	5	--
Blacke, Thomas	--	2	3	3	7	--
Backus, Philip	140	2	2	2	2	--
Bradford, Cha's	--	3	1	3	3	--
Boyars, And'w	300	2	3	10	7	--
Barker, John	100	2	2	3	5	--
Barker, Jos'h, Sen'r	70	1	2	1	2	--
Brown, Wm.	--	1	2	4	4	--
Brand, John	100	2	2	1	6	--

Franklyn Township

	Acres	Horses	Cattle	Sheep	White	Black
Brand, James	100	2	1	--	3	--
Burt, Jotham	200	1	3	11	7	--
Bartlett, Thomas	--	2	1	4	3	--
Boyers, John, single	100	2	1	--	1	--
Boyers, And'w, d'o	100	1	--	--	1	--
Battershell, Freeman, d'o	--	1	--	--	1	--
Boys, James, d'o	--	2	--	--	1	--
Boys, Rich'd, d'o	--	--	--	--	1	--
Best, Thomas, d'o	--	1	--	--	1	--
Berry, John, d'o	--	2	--	--	1	--
Battershell, John, d'o	80	--	--	--	--	--
Burt, Ebenezer	--	2	1	--	2	--
Barker, James	80	1	3	--	5	--
Crawford, James	--	1	1	7	5	--
Conners, Sam'l	--	--	--	2	11	--
Crawford, John	--	1	4	10	6	--
Chalfants, Chads	200	2	3	--	8	--
Carr, James	--	2	--	--	3	--
Chipely, Wm.	200	--	--	--	--	--
Cork, Benj'n	--	1	1	--	2	--
Crosley, David	--	--	--	--	--	--
Carson, Wm.	--	--	--	--	--	--
Cannon, Dan'l	300	4	7	12	8	--
Crawford, Widow	300	2	3	7	2	3
Crawford, Alex'r	--	2	4	12	7	--
Chain, Hugh	--	1	1	2	7	--
Cathcart, David	200	2	2	4	5	--
Cherry, John	150	2	2	5	10	--
Carson, John	100	2	2	2	4	--
Curry, Rob't	30	2	2	2	7	--
Carmical, John	300	2	2	4	5	--
Combs, Joseph	300	5	7	11	7	--
Cummins, John, single	50	1	--	--	5	--
Carson, Alex'r, d'o	--	1	1	--	1	--
Carson, W'm	150	2	5	12	9	--
Clemons, Jos'h	--	2	--	--	--	--
Campbell, Ja's	--	2	2	--	5	--
Carson, W'm, single	--	--	--	--	1	--
Dowden, Nath'l	--	2	--	--	3	--
Dawson, W'm	80	1	3	4	8	--
Dougharty, Jn'o	--	2	3	3	9	--
Dawson, Tho's	100	2	3	5	3	--
Davis, Benj'n	150	2	2	3	4	--
Dawson, Benoni	--	6	4	14	14	7
Dorson, John	300	2	2	5	5	--
Davis, John	--	1	2	--	10	--
Dunlap, Adam	300	2	3	2	6	--
Dunlap, Wm.	30	2	2	6	5	--
Dawson, John	--	1	2	3	5	--
Dunn, Thomas	200	2	2	--	10	--
Dunlap, John	150	2	2	4	3	--
Dugan, Rob't	60	3	2	6	6	--
Davis, Zach'h	100	2	3	6	7	--
Dickeson, Joshua	400	3	5	10	15	--
Davis, Thomas	400	3	4	5	6	--

Franklyn Township	Acres	Horses	Cattle	Sheep	White	Black
Dunlap, Sam'l, single	150	2	2	2	2	--
Davis, James, d'o	--	--	--	--	1	--
Dickson, Silas, d'o	--	--	--	--	1	--
Dickson, Stafford	--	2	2	--	1	--
Dagley, Mich'l, single	--	--	--	--	1	--
Dickson, Joseph	300	2	5	--	7	--
Estall, Thomas	100	2	2	--	4	--
Estall, Dan'l, single	--	--	--	--	1	--
Flud, Mich'l	100	1	2	1	3	--
Futhy, Sam'l	300	1	1	--	3	--
Finley, Sam'l	300	4	4	7	4	--
Freeman, Tho's	230	3	3	5	3	--
Forkner, Alex'r, single	--	--	--	--	1	--
Foster, Jeremiah, single	--	--	--	--	1	--
Fleming, Nath'l	100	2	3	3	7	--
Fulton, John, single	--	1	--	--	1	--
Forkner, David	100	1	2	9	5	--
Freeman, Sam'l	300	3	6	9	9	--
Garrat, John	--	2	2	N	10	--
Gorcham, John	--	2	3	3	3	1
Gibson, Wm.	--	1	2	3	8	--
Green, Lavor	150	2	3	5	4	--
Gilmore, Geo.	--	2	2	--	5	--
Gammell, Sam'l	200	1	1	--	4	--
Gibson, Jn'o	--	2	3	8	7	--
Gibson, Sam'l	150	1	2	3	7	--
Grier, Tho's	200	2	3	6	6	--
Gibson, Jn'o, Jun'r	--	1	1	--	3	--
Gibson, Edw'd	30	1	2	--	5	--
Gillilon, Henry	50	2	2	3	7	--
Gamble, Wm.	--	1	1	--	2	--
Golden, John	20	1	2	3	6	--
Gorcham, Tho's	--	4	9	11	10	6
Hanna, Marg't	--	1	2	--	5	--
Hardesty, Tho's	100	--	1	--	3	--
Hill, William	280	4	4	--	8	2
Harrison, Widow	300	2	6	6	9	3
Henry, Aaron	--	1	2	2	5	--
Hardisty, Francis	180	2	3	6	8	--
Hawthorn, Widow	80	1	1	--	8	--
Howard, Philip	100	2	1	--	9	--
Harrison, Charles	40	1	1	--	2	--
Harrison, Nich's	--	1	1	1	6	--
Harlain, James	--	2	2	--	3	--
Huston, John	300	1	1	1	4	--
Harper, James	300	2	2	3	9	--
Hull, Solomon	--	--	--	--	5	--
Hannon, Jn'o	40	1	1	2	2	--
Hendrix, Dan'l	--	2	2	--	4	--
Hendrix, Absalom	--	2	2	6	6	--
Hays, And'w	--	1	--	--	3	--
Hughey, Rob't	--	2	3	1	8	--
Hudd, John, single	80	1	--	--	1	--
Harkim, Peter, d'o	--	--	--	--	1	--
Hanna, Will'm, single	--	--	--	--	1	--

Franklyn Township	Acres	Horses	Cattle	Sheep	White	Black
Hall, Joseph	--	1	1	--	3	--
Harrison, Benj'n	300	1	1	1	4	--
Jourdan, Edw'd	80	2	3	5	9	--
Ireland, Jn'o	--	2	1	--	4	--
Jackson, Sam'l	300	5	4	--	6	--
Irwin, John	--	3	2	--	4	--
Johnston, Sam'l	300	2	4	6	5	--
John, John	500	2	3	6	8	--
Johnston, Arch'd	--	1	1	--	3	--
Irwin, Joseph, single	--	--	--	--	1	--
Keeling, Patrick	--	--	--	--	1	--
Knox, Jn'o	--	1	2	--	7	--
Keeling, Jn'o	--	1	--	--	1	--
Linsey, Anth'y	--	--	--	--	--	--
Lynch, James	150	2	2	3	2	1
Lynch, Sam'l	100	2	1	--	5	--
Linsey, Jolson, Jn'o	--	1	2	2	3	--
Laughlin, Peter	--	3	4	10	8	5
Lynn, And'w, Sen'r	--	1	1	5	3	--
Laughlin, Rob't	100	2	2	3	3	--
Laughlin, Ja's	200	2	2	3	5	1
Lewis, Jacob	--	2	1	--	4	--
Logan, Wm.	--	2	3	2	7	--
Lewis, Fra's	50	3	3	1	7	--
Lynch, Geo.	50	2	2	4	9	--
Lynn, Patrick, single	--	--	--	--	1	--
Lawson, John, d'o	--	--	--	--	1	--
Lich, Franc's, d'o	300	--	--	--	1	--
Lynn, James, d'o	300	--	--	--	1	--
Lynn, And'w, Jun'r	130	--	--	--	--	--
Lewis, Evans	--	1	1	3	4	--
Logan, Patrick	90	1	1	--	6	--
Lyon, John	--	1	2	4	4	--
Lawson, Tho's	300	3	4	12	7	--
Linch, Patrick	--	--	--	--	--	--
Linch, Jn'o, single	150	3	--	--	1	--
Measure, Thomas	50	2	2	2	6	--
More, Tho's, miller	--	1	2	--	8	--
Masterson, Hugh	220	3	4	4	8	--
Mitchell, Wm.	--	2	2	2	4	--
Miller, Wm.	280	4	6	9	10	--
Morland, Alex'r	300	3	4	--	3	--
McHaffy, Moses	--	1	1	--	11	--
McHaffy, Sam'l	--	1	1	2	3	--
Maxwell, Jn'o	45	1	2	2	7	--
McClelland, Jn'o	300	4	8	16	7	1
Murphy, Wm.	--	--	--	--	6	--
Morland, David	250	1	3	1	12	--
McCowan, Alex'r	150	2	2	1	6	--
McCowan, Jos'h	--	1	2	--	3	--
Murphy, Rob't	100	3	4	4	11	--
McIntire, Tho's	--	1	1	--	1	--
Morelin, Wm.	--	2	3	5	10	--
Moody, James	--	1	3	4	7	--
McNab, George	200	1	2	2	4	--

Franklyn Township	Acres	Horses	Cattle	Sheep	White	Black
McMullen, Jn'o	--	2	3	4	6	--
Mitchell, Ja's	--	2	3	4	5	--
McCowan, Jn'o	--	1	1	--	4	--
McCormack, Wm.	600	--	--	--	--	--
McCra, Wm.	--	1	1	3	--	--
Morris, Isaac	200	2	3	5	9	--
McCormack, Ja's	--	1	2	--	4	--
McClain, Dan'l	60	2	3	2	7	--
Meant, Math'w	--	2	2	2	5	--
McLaughlin, Jn'o	300	3	4	6	7	--
McCollister, Jn'o	--	2	2	2	2	--
McLaughlin, Rob't	450	4	6	10	10	--
McLain, John, single	--	1	--	--	1	--
McMullen, Sam'l, d'o	--	--	--	--	1	--
Morelan, Josiah, d'o	--	--	--	--	1	--
McNeal, Arthur, d'o	--	--	--	--	1	--
Maxwell, Wm., d'o	20	--	--	--	1	--
McMullen, Ja's, d'o	--	1	--	--	1	--
Moore, Thomas	220	3	5	3	4	3
McGwire, Patrick, single	--	--	--	--	1	--
Mollan, Wm.	50	1	1	--	3	--
Morland, Wm.	300	3	4	2	4	--
Nelson, Joseph	300	2	2	--	9	--
Norris, Joseph	300	2	2	--	9	--
Norris, Wm.	100	3	3	8	11	--
Neal, Widow	100	--	1	1	1	--
Noble, Rich'd	450	8	8	12	7	7
Neeley, Math'w	160	2	4	10	4	--
Nicholas, James	120	1	2	--	7	--
O'Finn, John	--	1	--	--	1	--
Orr, Wm., single	--	1	--	--	1	--
Owen, Wid'w	--	--	2	4	1	--
Pollan, Sam'l	--	2	2	--	5	--
Parker, Rob't	--	1	1	--	2	--
Power, Benj'n	--	3	4	7	9	--
Philips, Rich'd	--	--	2	--	5	--
Phips, Jn'o	80	2	1	3	3	--
Powell, James	334	3	3	2	3	--
Parks, David	--	2	2	1	6	--
Pollock, Wm.	60	2	1	--	4	--
Pierce, Elisha	300	6	9	20	14	--
Penny, Joseph	100	1	2	3	7	--
Price, Christ'r	50	--	1	--	3	--
Parish, Edw'd	60	--	3	8	4	--
Parish, Rich'd	--	--	2	4	2	--
Patterson, Tho's	90	5	5	9	6	--
Philips, Sam'l	100	2	2	--	6	--
Patterson, James	150	2	4	8	8	--
Purdy, John	250	3	4	11	10	--
Prather, Tho's	289	2	2	6	6	--
Pope, W'm, single	--	1	--	--	1	--
Pierce, Joseph, d'o	--	--	--	--	1	--
Powers, Eli, d'o	--	1	--	--	1	--
Powers, Ja's, d'o	--	2	1	--	1	--
Poursly, David, d'o	--	1	--	--	1	--

Franklyn Township	Acres	Horses	Cattle	Sheep	White	Black
Parris, Wm.	--	3	3	--	13	--
Perky, Chris'r	30	1	2	4	9	--
Patterson, Wm.	200	4	4	8	8	--
Parks, Sam'l, single	--	1	--	--	1	--
Patterson, Jn'o, d'o	100	1	--	--	1	--
Philips, Jonath'n	310	2	1	6	6	--
Quisenbury, Moses	200	4	4	15	10	--
Quisenbury, Wm.	--	1	2	--	2	--
Robertson, John	150	1	2	--	6	--
Robertson, Alex'r	100	2	2	3	3	--
Rogers, Tho's	300	3	7	10	10	--
Ramsey, Wm.	70	1	3	3	5	--
Reed, Wm.	--	2	2	2	9	--
Robertson, Wm.	--	2	1	4	4	--
Ross, Tasf	--	1	1	--	3	--
Ross, Wm.	--	2	3	--	5	--
Ross, Rob't	300	3	3	6	11	3
Robertson, Ja's	--	1	2	1	6	--
Ragan, Resen	300	1	3	--	6	--
Rankin, Sam'l	180	3	4	--	6	--
Richey, Sam'l	--	1	--	--	4	--
Richey, Math'w	50	1	1	--	3	--
Rhoi, Sam'l	300	1	2	--	2	--
Rankin, James	200	2	3	6	1	--
Robertson, Wm.	100	2	2	5	2	--
Richey, John, single	150	2	4	6	6	--
Rogers, Joseph, d'o	--	--	--	--	1	--
Rhay, Rich'd, d'o	100	--	2	--	1	--
Ricket, Philip	--	2	1	--	3	--
Reed, John	200	2	3	2	4	--
Rogers, Jn'o	--	2	1	--	5	--
Riggs, Nath'l, single	50	1	3	--	4	--
Shrieves, Sam'l	--	2	1	--	7	--
Stilts, Anth'y	--	--	1	--	9	--
Stull, Wm.	300	4	5	1	9	1
Studwill, Cha's	--	1	1	--	4	--
Sweak, George	300	2	2	4	5	--
Sweank, Jacob	--	1	2	3	3	--
Summerville, Fra's	300	3	4	6	7	--
Stevens, Dan'l	15	2	3	--	4	--
Scantlin, John	--	1	1	--	6	--
Smith, Wm.	--	3	2	5	2	--
Seward, Sam'l	300	2	2	4	6	--
Smart, Joseph	100	2	1	--	5	--
Steward, Wm.	360	2	5	3	11	--
Stevens, Benj'n	400	6	7	27	9	5
Shanklin, Geo.	--	2	2	--	5	--
Smith, Wm.	--	--	1	--	3	--
Smith, Wm., Corbet	--	--	2	--	4	--
Smith, Corbet	150	2	2	1	4	--
Seward, James	300	2	7	1	7	--
Stevens, Rich'd	200	4	2	--	3	--
Scott, Wm.	300	2	4	3	4	--
Shores, Rich'd	--	1	3	3	8	--
Simpson, Gilbert	50	6	6	22	10	--

Franklyn Township	Acres	Horses	Cattle	Sheep	White	Black
Sparks, Isaac	100	1	3	6	7	--
Strain, Sam'l	150	2	5	4	7	--
Steel, Adam, single	40	1	--	--	1	--
Still, Wm., d'o	--	1	--	--	1	--
Smith, Andrew, d'o	--	--	--	--	1	--
Stevens, Joseph, d'o	--	1	--	--	1	--
Stuard, Jn'o	300	2	1	5	5	--
Sparks, Wm.	300	2	3	7	9	--
Stevens, Sam'l	500	2	1	--	1	--
Shearer, John, single	--	2	--	--	1	--
Taylor, Wm.	--	1	3	7	6	1
Tetrick, Jn'o	--	1	--	--	2	--
Travis, Jn'o	100	2	2	2	9	--
Thompson, James	50	2	2	2	5	--
Thompson, Nathan, single	--	1	1	--	1	--
Tarrance, Hugh	50	1	1	--	--	--
Tarrance, Sam'l	--	2	2	--	4	--
Tarrance, Joseph	30	2	1	1	4	--
Vankirk, Jacob	50	1	1	--	--	--
Wallis, Wm., single	--	--	--	--	1	--
Washington, his Excll'y	1,600	--	--	--	--	--
Watson, Rob't	--	1	1	--	4	--
Wilkey, James	300	3	3	6	11	--
Work, Joseph	300	2	2	2	5	--
Wells, Jn'o	60	2	1	--	9	3
Ward, Jn'o	--	1	3	3	6	--
Welsh, Cha's Tho's	--	1	2	2	4	--
Wilson, David	300	1	1	2	8	--
Wiley, Math'w	250	4	5	8	9	--
Willis, Rob't	30	3	3	5	5	--
Writtenhouse, Wm.	150	2	3	--	5	--
Wilson, Wm.	100	2	3	4	4	--
Washington, Jn'o, Col.	320	--	--	--	--	--
Work, Sam'l	300	3	4	6	7	--
Wells, Tunis	150	3	3	6	8	--
Young, Isaac	--	1	2	1	4	--
Young, James	--	--	1	--	7	--
Young, George	250	2	4	10	9	--
Young, Joseph	100	2	3	4	7	--
Young, Dan'l	75	2	2	--	1	--
Young, Charles	--	1	1	1	4	--
Total Inhabitants	--	--	--	--	1,661	52

Tyrone Township

	Acres	Horses	Cattle	Sheep	Inhabitants White	Black
Agnew, Ja's	--	3	3	6	10	--
Agnew, Isaac, single	--	--	--	--	1	--
Bealer, Chris'r	300	3	4	11	4	--
Boyd, Jn'o	--	1	3	1	6	--
Brewer, Benj'n	150	1	2	--	6	--

Tyrone Township	Acres	Horses	Cattle	Sheep	White	Black
Brewer, Sam'l	--	1	1	--	2	--
Bowers, Rob't, single	--	1	2	--	4	--
Bell, Jn'o, d'o	--	1	--	--	1	--
Bell, Jos'h, d'o	--	--	--	--	1	--
Bell, Sam'l	--	2	3	--	8	--
Butler, Edw'd	50	2	2	2	5	--
Berry, Jn'o, single	--	1	--	--	1	--
Brown, Wm.	--	1	2	--	8	--
Bourns, Ja's	--	1	2	4	4	--
Beall, Rob't	800	5	5	10	7	--
Blakly, Wm., single	--	--	--	--	1	--
Christy, John	300	--	--	--	--	--
Chain, Jn'o	--	2	--	--	3	--
Clifford, Cha's	50	--	2	6	9	--
Cavenaugh, Jn'o	--	--	1	--	2	--
Cunningham, Marg't	--	2	3	4	10	--
Cunningham, Bar'd	150	3	4	5	10	--
Clifford, Geo.	--	2	--	--	3	--
Chain, Wm.	--	2	2	3	2	--
Clark, Rich'd	--	2	1	2	7	--
Caint, Abs'm	60	2	2	5	5	--
Copper, Jos'h	--	2	2	--	8	--
Coyl, Manasah, single	--	1	--	--	1	--
Copper, Cha's, d'o	--	--	--	--	1	--
Campbell, Ja's	--	2	1	--	2	--
Connell, Zach'h	600	8	5	16	8	--
Curry, Tho's	--	1	2	--	8	--
Connell, Ann	300	2	6	10	5	--
Caldwell, Isaac	--	2	3	6	3	--
Clifford, Rob't, single	--	--	--	--	1	--
Cunningham, Jn'o, single	--	--	--	--	1	--
Curry, Myrack, d'o	--	--	--	--	1	--
Curry, Aeneas, d'o	--	--	--	--	1	--
Cornwall, Widow	200	1	2	--	1	--
Demus, Peter	--	2	2	--	5	--
Dunn, Nehem'h	100	2	3	4	2	--
Dunn, Hugh	--	--	1	--	9	--
Dummit, Wm.	100	1	1	--	7	--
Donoldson, Jn'o, single	--	--	--	--	1	--
Dyal, Edw'd	336	8	11	21	8	--
Davids, Tho's	50	2	3	11	6	--
Espy, Wm.	300	1	2	--	1	--
Evans, Henry	--	1	2	--	5	--
Erwin, Joseph	--	3	2	--	6	--
Evans, Jacob	--	1	1	--	7	--
Flemming, Rob't	--	2	3	10	12	--
Forsythe, Tho's	200	2	3	5	6	--
Flemming, Lewis	50	1	1	--	2	--
Flemming, Tho's	--	2	1	2	9	--
Furser, Geo., single	--	4	--	--	1	--
Flynn, Wm.	--	1	1	--	6	--
Garner, Ab'm	--	2	2	--	6	--
Gost, Craft	--	2	2	10	3	--
Graham, Rich'd	200	4	3	12	9	--
Graham, Noble, single	--	1	--	--	1	--

Tyrone Township

	Acres	Horses	Cattle	Sheep	White	Black
Gaut, Math'w	--	1	1	6	7	--
Glasgow, Sam'l	300	2	1	6	4	--
Garner, Edw'd, single	--	--	--	--	1	--
Graham, David	--	2	2	--	5	--
Hunter, Cyrus, single	--	1	--	--	1	--
Hutchison, Rebecca	300	1	1	1	9	--
Huston, Wm., single	--	--	--	--	6	--
Huston, Marg't	--	1	1	1	1	--
Hicks, Sam'l	--	2	4	5	4	--
Haslep, Ja's	50	2	2	7	3	--
Hodge, Jn'o	--	1	2	--	3	--
Happy, Ja's	--	2	1	--	5	--
Huey, Tho's, single	--	--	--	--	1	--
Hatfield, Adam	300	--	2	--	7	--
Hickman, Fra's	12	2	2	6	3	--
Hickman, Eliz'a	300	3	4	3	3	--
Hite, Sarah	300	--	--	--	--	--
Hickman, Tram'l, single	--	1	--	--	1	--
Jones, Philip	--	2	2	--	7	--
Johnson, Henry	100	2	2	4	8	--
Johnson, Ja's & Roger	100	2	3	3	10	--
Jump, Jn'o	--	2	1	2	4	--
Kesler, Peter	50	1	2	7	6	--
Loudon, Tho's	300	2	2	1	2	--
Linn, Sam'l	--	2	1	--	7	--
Levy, Isaac	--	1	1	--	3	--
Loury, Jn'o	--	3	4	4	6	--
Lindsey, David	100	3	4	9	9	--
Lindsey, Edm'd	200	2	2	8	9	--
Mason, Isaac	500	7	7	8	7	--
Minor, Jn'o	--	1	2	3	8	--
Mathews, Jn'o	--	2	4	8	4	--
Mason, Jn'o, Maj.	300	4	5	8	7	--
Mason, Joseph, single	300	--	--	--	1	--
Meeks, Jacob	300	1	2	2	6	--
Martin, Jn'o	100	2	2	--	4	--
Morecraft, Jn'o	100	3	1	5	6	--
Means, Jn'o	--	1	1	--	5	--
Murphy, Pat'k, single	--	2	2	--	2	--
Mintor, Jn'o	1,100	3	5	9	5	--
Murphy, Sam'l, single	--	1	--	--	1	--
Morrison, Jn'o	--	2	2	4	2	--
Morgan, George	300	--	--	--	--	--
Messor, Hugh	840	--	--	--	--	--
Martain, Tho's	--	1	1	--	4	--
Mounts, Providence	1,000	6	9	15	9	--
Millegan, Ja's	--	2	2	--	7	--
Mason, Philip	300	2	2	10	9	--
McHafaty, Jn'o	--	2	2	--	6	--
Mounts, Provid'e, single	--	1	--	--	1	--
McKinley, David	50	2	2	--	4	--
Massey, Wm.	300	2	2	10	6	--
McCullough, David	--	1	1	--	2	--
McKee, Wm.	250	4	4	16	7	--
McIntire, Jn'o	50	--	2	2	5	--

Tyrone Township	Acres	Horses	Cattle	Sheep	White	Black
McClintic, Alex'r	50	2	2	4	5	--
Massey, Jn'o, single	--	--	--	--	1	--
Mason, Jn'o, d'o	--	--	--	--	1	--
Neesbit, Jn'o	--	2	3	1	6	--
Neesbit, Nath., single	--	--	--	--	1	--
Neesbit, Sam'l	--	2	2	--	5	--
Porter, Jn'o	--	2	5	--	9	--
Porter, Rob't, single	--	1	--	--	1	--
Pierce, Isaac	--	--	1	--	7	--
Perry, David	300	3	5	8	5	--
Parkill, David	280	2	4	--	4	--
Piper, James, single	--	--	--	--	1	--
Rogers, Geo.	--	2	3	6	9	--
Roze, Enoch	--	1	3	1	11	--
Rudibaugh, Chris'r	50	2	2	--	3	--
Ray, Henry	300	2	1	2	7	--
Rhodes, Henry	150	3	4	5	11	--
Right, Jn'o	--	2	3	6	5	--
Rayburn, Rob't	--	1	1	2	5	--
Rice, Edm'd	353	3	4	6	7	--
Ragan, Garard, single	--	1	--	--	1	--
Studiberger, Peter	210	2	2	--	3	--
Statia, Peter	250	1	2	--	5	--
Smith, Wm.	300	1	1	--	6	--
Steward, Ja's, single	--	--	--	--	1	--
Steward, Rob't, d'o	--	--	--	--	1	--
Steward, Wm.	50	2	3	--	6	--
Smiley, Jn'o	300	3	4	13	5	--
Snodgrass, Sam'l	--	1	2	--	5	--
Secrets, Valentine	300	2	3	4	7	--
Steward, John	250	2	2	1	12	--
Steward, David	90	1	1	--	9	--
Stevenson, John	350	4	7	12	3	--
Smith, David	--	2	2	2	6	--
Statia, Tho's, single	--	1	--	--	1	--
Stevenson, Ja's	--	4	4	9	6	--
Stevenson, Marcus	--	2	2	4	7	--
Smith, Moses	600	2	3	3	8	--
Smith, Wm., single	--	--	--	--	1	--
Smith, Mich'l, d'o	--	--	--	--	1	--
Thompson, Henry	--	2	3	4	5	--
Thompson, Rob't, single	--	--	--	--	1	--
Tarrance, James	250	2	3	2	6	--
Trimble, Ja's, single	--	1	--	--	1	--
Vernon, Jn'o	--	3	3	--	1	--
Vanderen, Jn'o	300	--	--	--	--	--
Vance, Marg't	300	2	2	3	6	--
Waram, Jn'o	250	4	6	5	6	--
Waram, Ja's	200	1	1	--	2	--
Whiteside, Joseph	100	2	3	--	5	--
Walters, Jn'o	50	2	1	1	2	--
Whitesides, Wm.	--	2	3	--	3	--
Whitesides, Sam'l	200	--	--	--	--	--
Wilson, Benj'n	--	1	1	--	5	--
Wilson, And'w, single	--	--	--	--	1	--

Tyrone Township	Acres	Horses	Cattle	Sheep	White	Black
White, Moses	300	1	1	3	4	--
Wells, Benj'n	--	2	4	1	6	--
Walker, Henry	--	1	1	--	3	--
White, Wm., single	--	1	--	--	1	--
White, Henry	150	3	5	6	11	--
White, Jn'o	--	2	2	3	4	--
White, Wm.	200	2	4	4	--	--
White, Isaac	--	2	1	2	--	--
Waugh, Paul	--	2	4	6	7	--
Whaley, Ja's, single	--	--	--	--	1	--
Wilson, Sam'l	300	2	1	--	2	--
Young, Nathan	--	1	1	--	5	--
Total Inhabitants	--	--	--	--	816	--

Derry Township

	Acres	Horses	Cattle	Sheep	Inhabitants White	Black
Allison -----	150	--	--	--	--	--
Allison, And'w	200	2	2	--	--	--
Allis, Jn'o	150	1	1	--	--	--
Allis, Mark	100	3	2	--	--	--
Anderson, David	300	--	--	--	--	--
Anderson, -----	300	--	--	--	--	--
Anderson, -----	300	--	--	--	--	--
Anderson, -----	300	--	--	--	--	--
Bogel, -----	100	--	--	--	--	--
Baird, Ja's	300	--	--	--	--	--
Barr, Ja's	300	2	3	6	--	--
Barr, Alex'r	300	2	3	--	--	--
Bear, Jn'o	--	2	1	--	--	--
Brown, Wm.	200	2	2	--	--	--
Burns, James	200	--	--	--	--	--
Brown, -----	300	--	--	--	--	--
Bears, Fred'k	200	--	--	--	--	--
Brooks, Aaron	100	--	--	--	--	--
Barr, Mary	200	--	--	--	--	--
Boyd, Jn'o	100	--	--	--	--	--
Baird, Cha's	200	2	2	--	--	--
Baird, Moses	100	2	1	--	--	--
Barihill, Alex'r	300	--	--	--	--	--
Bently, Mary	100	--	--	--	--	--
Blane, Widow	300	--	--	--	--	--
Caldwell, Jn'o	30	2	2	2	--	--
Chapman, Nich's	200	2	2	2	--	--
Craig, Jn'o	200	2	1	--	--	--
Campbell, Ja's	300	--	--	--	--	--
Carroll, Ja's	40	--	--	--	--	--
Crow, Jn'o	200	--	--	--	--	--
Cahill, Edw'd	900	1	2	--	--	--
Cahill, Edw'd, Jun'r	300	--	--	--	--	--
Culbertson, -----	100	--	--	--	--	--

Derry Township

Name	Acres	Horses	Cattle	Sheep	White	Black
Campbell, -----	100	--	--	--	--	--
Campbell, Ja's	100	--	--	--	--	--
Campbell, Wm.	100	2	2	--	--	--
Campbell, Jn'o	100	--	--	--	--	--
Caldwell, Wm.	200	--	--	--	--	--
Cochran, Wm.	300	2	2	5	--	--
Cortney, Wm.	200	--	--	--	--	--
Cleghorn, Math'w	150	2	1	--	--	--
Cleghorn, Jn'o	150	2	1	--	--	--
Carr, James	200	--	--	--	--	--
Caldwell, Rob't	100	--	--	--	--	--
Curry, Wm.	300	--	--	--	--	--
Clark, Ja's	300	--	--	--	--	--
Craig, Sam'l	300	1	--	--	--	--
Craig, Jean	300	2	3	12	--	--
Clasky, Rob't	--	2	3	--	--	--
Clark, Geo.	200	--	--	--	--	--
Crozier, Wm.	100	2	3	--	--	--
Dennison, Jn'o	300	--	--	--	--	--
Dennison, Arth'r	300	4	5	10	--	--
Donahe, Jn'o	100	--	--	--	--	--
Donold, -----	100	--	--	--	--	--
Donoldson, Isaac	100	--	--	--	--	--
Dunlap, Wm.	100	2	2	2	--	--
Dickson, Jos'h	200	--	--	--	--	--
Donold, Moses	300	3	6	9	--	--
Donold, James	300	--	--	--	--	--
English, Ja's	100	--	--	--	--	--
Eaton, Ja's	100	2	2	--	--	--
Eckles, Wm.	100	--	--	--	--	--
Erwin, Sam'l	300	--	--	--	--	--
Feals, Alex'r	100	--	--	--	--	--
Flemming, Jn'o	--	2	2	--	--	--
Fulton, Ja's	100	--	--	--	--	--
Guthrie, Wm.	300	2	2	--	--	--
Glen, James	100	--	--	--	--	--
Gallahar, Ja's	100	--	--	--	--	--
Gallahar, Barney	300	--	--	--	--	--
Guthrie, Alex'r	100	--	--	--	--	--
Girts, Harmon	100	3	3	4		
Girts, Henry	80	--	--	--	--	--
Hughs, Wm.	200	3	3	4	--	--
Hutabaugh, Geo.	100	2	1	--	--	--
Harbridge, Edw'd	100	--	--	--	--	--
Hall, Ja's	300	2	1	--	--	--
Henry, Rob't	100	--	--	--	--	--
Jolly, Tho's	300	2	2	--	--	--
Joice, Wm.	100	2	4	--	--	--
Kilpatrick, Sam'l	--	3	2	--	--	--
Kelly, Edw'd	100	--	--	--	--	--
Kilpatrick, Dan'l	200	--	--	--	--	--
Lowers, Rob't	150	--	--	--	--	--
Latta, Eph'm	100	--	--	--	--	--
Love, Wm.	500	--	--	--	--	--
Leonard, James	--	1	1	--	--	--

Derry Township	Acres	Horses	Cattle	Sheep	White	Black
Lazure, Geo.	100	2	4	9	--	--
Lambert, Jn'o	200	--	1	--	--	--
Lasley, Jn'o	--	2	3	--	--	--
Mathews, Ezekiel	--	1	2	1	--	--
Maxwell, Adam	200	--	--	--	--	--
Mann, Joseph	100	2	2	4	--	--
Millar, Rob't	--	2	1	--	--	--
Mitchell, Wm.	300	2	2	--	--	--
Mitchell, Wm., Sen'r	300	--	--	--	--	--
McIntire, -----	300	--	--	--	--	--
McIntire, And'w	100	--	--	--	--	--
McClean, Ja's	--	2	3	--	--	--
McClean, Alex'r	300	3	3	--	--	--
McColister, Alex'r	100	1	1	--	--	--
McColister, Ja's	100	1	1	--	--	--
McClean, Alex.	100	1	1	--	--	--
McCrady, Jn'o	300	2	2	2	--	--
Peterson, -----	300	--	--	--	--	--
Patton, Wm.	300	--	--	--	--	--
Patterson, Sam'l	300	3	3	--	--	--
Patrick, Jn'o	100	2	1	--	--	--
Pettit, Elias	200	--	--	--	--	--
Perry, Wm.	100	--	--	--	--	--
Parr, Isaac	300	2	3	3	--	--
Parr, James	100	2	1	--	--	--
Parr, Sam'l	300	1	--	--	--	--
Pomroy, Jn'o	600	2	1	2	--	--
Reynolds, Jn'o	150	--	--	--	--	--
Russell, James	100	--	--	--	--	--
Russell, Jn'o	200	--	--	--	--	--
Rount, Jacob	100	2	2	--	--	--
Ramsey, -----	200	--	--	--	--	--
Steward, And'w	150	2	1	--	--	--
Sarren, Sam'l	--	2	2	--	--	--
Stevenson, Wm.	100	1	1	--	--	--
Smirl, Geo.	100	2	3	3	--	--
Stevenson, Tho's	150	2	2	3	--	--
Stevenson, Ja's	150	1	1	--	--	--
Stevenson, Jean	150	2	1	--	--	--
Smith, -----	300	--	--	--	--	--
Sloan, Sam'l	200	4	5	12	--	--
Scott, -----	200	--	--	--	--	--
Scott, Ja's	40	--	--	--	--	--
Skinner, -----	200	--	--	--	--	--
Sloan, Jn'o	250	1	--	--	--	--
Soxman, Chris'n	200	2	3	7	--	--
Smith, Rob't	100	2	2	--	--	--
Stockberger, Mich'l	200	--	--	--	--	--
Thompson, Ja's	300	3	5	9	--	--
Taylor, Rob't	200	3	3	5	--	--
Tanner, Wm.	--	2	1	--	--	--
Thompson, Anth'y	200	3	2	2	--	--
Taylor, Thomas	300	2	3	--	--	--
Thompson, Jn'o	100	2	1	--	--	--
Tinnel, Wm.	100	2	1	--	--	--

Derry Township	Acres	Horses	Cattle	Sheep	White	Black
Voras, Ralph	300	4	4	10	--	--
Wallis, Rich'd	300	2	2	4	--	--
Wilson, Jos'h	--	2	2	--	--	--
Waddle, Sam'l	140	--	--	--	--	--
Woolf, And'w	50	--	--	--	--	--
Wilkey, Thomas	200	--	--	--	--	--
Wilson, James	300	2	2	3	--	--
Wills, Ja's	150	--	--	--	--	--
Wills, And'w	150	--	--	--	--	--
Wallis, Ja's	150	2	3	6	--	--
Watson, Wm.	200	--	--	--	--	--

Pitt Township

	Acres	Horses	Cattle	Sheep		
Amberson, Wm.	--	--	1	--	--	--
Bell, Tho's	--	--	--	--	--	--
Beaty, Jos'h	300	--	--	--	--	--
Barr, Jn'o	500	2	2	--	--	--
Burrows, Ja's	40	2	3	4	--	--
Buhar, Chris'n, single	150	3	1	3	--	--
Burkart, Jacob	100	2	2	1	--	--
Bishop, Wm.	--	1	1	--	--	--
Brady, Wm.	--	--	--	--	--	--
Brackinridge, Hugh, single	--	1	1	--	--	--
Boggs, James, d'o	--	--	1	--	--	--
Brannon, Peter	--	1	2	--	--	--
Bradly, Jn'o	--	1	1	--	--	--
Croghan, Geo.	600	--	--	--	--	--
Chambers, Ja's	169	3	3	--	--	--
Carroll, Tho's, single	200	--	--	--	--	--
Craig, Tho's	--	1	1	--	--	--
Cameron, Gilbert	--	1	1	--	--	--
Carmical, Jn'o	--	1	2	1	--	--
Cunningham, Wm.	100	3	4	3	--	--
Campbell, Rob't, single	--	1	--	1	--	--
Casselman, Jacob	600	3	4	--	--	--
Clark, Jn'o, single	--	2	3	--	--	--
Cristy, Wm.	200	1	2	--	--	--
Chambers, Tho's, single	--	--	--	--	--	--
Cranmore, Agnes	--	--	--	--	--	--
Campbell, Jn'o	300	--	--	--	--	--
Collins, Jn'o	--	1	--	--	--	--
Duncan, David	300	5	6	--	--	--
Dunbar, Jn'o	100	2	3	5	--	--
Davis, Hugh	350	--	--	--	--	--
Duke, Cha's	250	2	3	--	--	--
Dougharty, Martha	200	1	2	--	--	--
Donoldson, Hugh	--	2	1	--	--	--
Dunfield, Fred'k	--	1	2	--	--	--
Dunning, Rob't	4	1	2	1	--	--
Deal, Wm.	--	2	2	--	--	--

Pitt Township   Acres Horses Cattle Sheep

Name	Acres	Horses	Cattle	Sheep		
Davis, Mary	--	--	--	--	--	--
Douglass, And'w	--	1	--	--	--	--
Dousman, Jn'o	--	2	--	--	--	--
Douglass, Eph'm	300	--	--	--	--	--
Evans, Wm., single	--	--	--	--	--	--
Evalt, Sam'l	200	2	2	--	--	--
Elliot, Wm.	1,400	4	3	--	--	--
Fernsly, James	100	3	3	--	--	--
Frazier, Rory	--	2	1	--	--	--
Ferry, Widow	300	--	--	--	--	--
Finley, Jos'h	200	--	--	--	--	--
Francis, Philip, single	--	--	--	--	--	--
Flemming, Ja's	200	2	4	10	--	--
Fowler, Alex'r	--	5	2	2	--	--
Ferree, Jn'o	250	1	2	3	--	--
Freeman, Wm., single	--	--	--	--	--	--
Flinn, Wm.	--	3	--	--	--	--
Guffy, Henry	30	2	3	--	--	--
Guffy, Ja's	50	2	2	--	--	--
Grames, Peter	200	2	1	--	--	--
Glass, Jn'o	200	1	2	--	--	--
Gibson, Tho's	--	2	--	--	--	--
Grimes, Donold	--	2	--	--	--	--
Gunn, Wm., single	--	1	1	--	--	--
Grubb, Jacob	--	1	1	--	--	--
Girty, Tho's	300	1	2	--	--	--
Girty, Jn'o	--	2	2	--	--	--
Gibson, Jn'o	--	2	2	--	--	--
Galbreath, Rob't	--	1	1	1	--	--
Hamilton, Arch'd	--	1	2	--	--	--
Holmes, Jon'a, single	--	--	--	--	--	--
Hamilton, Jn'o	--	2	2	--	--	--
Handlyn, Jn'o	--	1	--	--	--	--
Huffnagle, Mical	600	1	--	--	--	--
Haymaker, Jacob	300	--	--	--	--	--
Heth, Henry	300	--	--	--	--	--
Hagarty, Nich's	--	--	--	--	--	--
Johnston, Jn'o	150	2	2	--	--	--
Irwin, Jn'o, Sen'r	15	1	2	--	--	--
Irwin, Agnes	150	2	1	1	--	--
Irwin, Jn'o, Jun'r, single	--	3	--	--	--	--
Irwin, David	--	1	1	--	--	--
Johnson, Benj'n	--	--	--	--	--	--
Kyser, Benj'n	60	2	3	9	--	--
Karr, Martha	--	--	1	--	--	--
Kinkead, James	--	--	--	--	--	--
Keasy, James	--	1	--	--	--	--
Linehart, Chris'n	300	1	1	--	--	--
Lane, Isaac	40	2	8	--	--	--
Lightenberger, Geo.	--	3	1	--	--	--
Lazure, Hiat	--	--	1	--	--	--
McKay, Mary	930	2	2	--	--	--
Myers, James	250	1	2	5	--	--
Myers, Eliez'r	300	2	4	4	--	--
McBride, Tho's	--	2	1	--	--	--

Pitt Township   Acres Horses Cattle Sheep

Name	Acres	Horses	Cattle	Sheep	
Miles, Tho's	300	--	--	--	--
McGoldrick, Ja's	250	--	--	--	--
McGinnis, Cha's	300	4	2	1	--
McDonald, Jn'o	200	1	2	1	--
McDonold, Dan'l	--	1	--	--	--
McCloud, Murdock	--	1	2	5	--
McCartney, Peter	200	2	2	--	--
McLain, Laughlin	--	1	1	--	--
McDonold, Hugh	--	2	1	--	--
McElroy, Widow	10	--	2	--	--
Millegen, Ja's	130	2	4	--	--
McKee, Jn'o	200	--	--	--	--
McClelland, Ja's	--	1	1	--	--
McElwane, Fra's	--	1	3	--	--
McDonold, Pat'k	200	2	2	--	--
Murphy, Pat'k	--	3	1	--	--
Millar, Eliz'a	300	1	1	--	--
Miller, Jn'o	--	2	--	--	--
Martin, Wm.	--	--	--	--	--
McKinley, Rob't	--	--	--	--	--
Neal, Rob't	200	2	1	--	--
Naugle, And'w, single	--	1	--	--	--
Negley, Alex'r	100	1	1	--	--
Nicholason, Jos'h	--	2	2	8	--
Ormsby, Jn'o	--	3	3	4	--
O'Hara, Hugh	10	2	2	--	--
Owins, Wm.	--	--	2	--	--
O'Harra, Ja's	--	--	--	--	--
Pollock, James	300	--	--	--	--
Powell, Wm.	300	4	5	6	--
Powell, Wm., Jun'r, single	300	--	--	--	--
Powell, Ja's	200	--	--	--	--
Phillips, Tho's	--	1	2	--	--
Parchment, Nich's	--	1	2	1	--
Parchment, Peter	--	1	1	--	--
Quigley, Hugh	300	2	4	--	--
Robinson, James, single	--	1	--	--	--
Rysor, Dan'l	600	--	--	--	--
Ryan, Ja's	300	2	5	2	--
Roleter, Peter	350	3	4	3	--
Rybolt, Jacob	200	--	--	--	--
Rodearmor, Jn'o	600	2	6	4	--
Rinehart, And'w	100	4	9	13	--
Riddin, Wm.	70	2	3	--	--
Ruddin, Wm.	70	2	3	--	--
Reed, James	140	2	3	1	--
Ryan, Jacob	--	1	1	--	--
Rynaman, Chr'r	--	2	1	5	--
Reed, Ja's, Jun'r	600	1	--	--	--
Rammage, Wm.	200	3	3	5	--
Ramage, Jn'o	--	2	1	3	--
Rankin, Sol'o	--	1	3	--	--
Reel, Gasper, single	--	1	1	--	--
Ross, Tho's	300	--	--	--	--
Riddick, Wm.	--	1	1	--	--

Pitt Township	Acres	Horses	Cattle	Sheep
Simons, Jos'h	1,218	--	--	--
Simons & Millegan	--	--	--	--
Smallman & Ward	--	--	--	--
Smith, Deverux	850	4	2	--
D'o, d'o	310	--	--	--
Smith, Doctor	300	--	--	--
Simmerman, Mich'l	300	--	--	--
St. Clair, Gen'l	300	--	--	--
Smallman, Tho's	300	2	4	--
Sheanor, Mathias	--	--	--	--
Shepherd, Edw'd	--	--	--	--
Strain, Mich'l	200	2	1	--
Sample, Sam'l	285	2	3	1
Thompson, James	--	1	1	--
Troop, Widow	100	1	2	3
Thompson, Jn'o, single	--	--	--	--
Trent, -----	50	--	--	--
Tannihill, Adam'n	--	--	--	--
Terret, Cha's	--	--	--	--
Thompson, Gen'l, heirs	600	--	--	--
Valentine, Wm.	300	2	2	5
Ward, Edw'd	6	1	2	--
Wilson, Wm., single	--	1	1	--
Whitgar, Ab'm	300	--	--	--
Whitsel, Jacob	300	2	2	--
Winemiller, Jacob	230	2	4	3
Winemiller, Coonrod	600	--	--	--
Williams, Jn'o	--	1	--	--
White, Jn'o	200	2	3	1
Whitesell, Barbara	200	1	1	5
Wise, Jacob	40	2	2	4
Winebiddle, Conrad	300	2	2	3
Wilson, Tho's	200	5	6	7
Wilson, Fra's	320	4	--	--
Wallis, Geo.	10	2	3	--
Watson, James	--	--	--	--
Wilson, Col's heirs	--	--	--	--
Richards, Cha's	--	1	2	--
Robinson, And'w	--	2	1	5
Evalt, Sam'l	30	--	--	--
Bennet, Benj'n	--	1	1	--
Bennet, Benj'n, Jun'r	--	1	1	--
Millar, Wm.	--	--	1	--

Hempfield Township	Acres	Horses	Cattle	Sheep
Allimong, Nich'w	300	2	2	--
Altman, Will'm	300	3	4	6
Altman, Peter, black	250	2	5	--
Arrat, Christian	300	2	4	4
Altman, Peter, white	260	2	3	4

Hempfield Township	Acres	Horses	Cattle	Sheep
Altman, Anthony	268	--	8	5
Altman, Gasper	--	2	2	--
Alexander, Hugh	100	2	2	2
Ammon, George	100	1	2	2
Arrat, John	--	2	2	--
Barnhart, Will'm	100	1	3	--
Barnhart, Jacob	--	1	1	--
Brown, Jn'o, Jun'r	--	2	1	--
Beaty, Sam'l	--	2	4	10
Barns, Will'm	--	2	3	--
Brown, -----	300	--	--	--
Brown, Will'm	300	2	2	4
Baum, Chris'n	250	4	2	4
Briny, Peter	100	2	1	--
Beaty, Wm.	--	1	--	--
Best, Wm.	250	2	3	--
Bell, Wm.	150	2	3	2
Byars, Geo.	100	3	3	2
Bush, Dan'l	100	2	2	--
Bovaird, Ja's	100	2	2	--
Boyd, Darcus	300	--	--	--
Brown, Jn'o, Sen'r	250	2	2	--
Best, Rob't	--	2	1	--
Brownlee, Hugh	300	1	--	--
Bryson, James	--	1	--	--
Brannon, Wm.	--	2	1	--
Brannon, Jn'o	--	2	1	2
Brisby, Wm.	50	1	1	--
Calgan, Pat'k	--	1	--	--
Cooper, Will'm	--	1	--	--
Conkle, Mich'l	400	4	6	7
Christy, Jn'o	--	2	2	--
Crookshanks, And'w	300	2	3	4
Cherry, Peter	20	1	1	--
Culberson, Jn'o	--	1	1	--
Crips, Jn'o	--	1	2	4
Clinglesmith, Dan'l	150	3	3	6
Clinglesmith, Philip	--	--	--	--
Caple, Jacob	300	2	3	2
Camara, John	250	3	4	2
Conkle, Jn'o	450	3	3	3
Clinglesmith, Peter, Jun'r	100	2	2	--
Camera, Adam	--	1	--	--
Clinglesmith, And'w	--	2	2	--
Camara, Ludwick	250	1	--	--
Clinglesmith, Peter, Dec'd	--	1	2	2
Carnahan, David	--	1	1	--
Cook, Cath'e	100	2	1	1
Clinglesmith, Jn'o	--	1	--	--
Conway, Hugh	--	2	2	--
Callan, Will'm	200	3	3	6
Clinglesmith, Pet'r, single	100	2	2	--
Carrol, James	--	2	2	3
Cooper, Sam'l	50	2	4	6
Drum, Simon	150	2	3	--

Hempfield Township   Acres Horses Cattle Sheep

	Acres	Horses	Cattle	Sheep
Davis, Hanover	300	3	5	5
Dedor, Jacob	--	2	--	--
Dunkan, Ja's, single	--	1	--	--
Everer, Adam	--	2	--	--
Elsworth, And'w	400	--	--	--
Everet, Jacob	160	1	1	1
Finley, James	--	1	--	--
Fulton, Jn'o	300	--	--	--
Freetly, Jacob, single	--	1	--	--
Freetly, Martani	--	2	--	--
Foreman, Cha's, Esq'r	300	2	2	5
Freeman, Adam	--	1	--	--
Freeman, Wm.	--	1	2	2
Freeman, Tho's	200	2	3	4
Fleming, Rob't	200	2	4	8
Faries, James	200	3	4	2
Fritchman, Adam	200	2	5	6
George, Adam	300	3	2	5
Gallaher, Eman'l	--	2	2	--
Gross, Chris'n	300	2	3	8
Groushour, John	300	2	2	5
Grous, Peter	200	2	3	8
Huffnagle, Mich'l	--	--	--	--
Hill, -----	200	--	--	--
Hanna, Rob't	240	4	--	--
Haseley, Henry	160	2	2	--
Huffnagle, Mich'l, Esq'r	190	--	--	--
Hilands, Barney	--	2	3	--
Harold, Chr'r, Sen'r	300	2	5	10
Harman, Peter	--	2	--	--
Harold, Peter	300	3	2	2
Harold, John	250	3	4	2
Houser, John	300	2	3	3
Hawk, Coonrad	300	4	4	5
Henry, Fre'k	250	3	2	6
Hill, Peter	--	2	1	--
Hutabaugh, Geo.	--	2	2	2
Harold, Chr'r, Jun'r	100	2	2	--
Hays, John	--	2	1	--
Hamson, Will'm	--	2	4	6
Hughs, Jn'o, Esq'r	300	6	3	8
Hall, Rob't	200	2	2	3
Hoak, And'w	--	1	2	--
Hoak, Sam'l	300	2	2	--
Harman, Peter	--	2	--	--
Hunter, Rob't	--	2	2	1
Jackson, John	--	3	2	2
Irwin, Lau'ce	300	2	2	--
Iceman, Peter	300	3	2	2
Irwin, Jn'o	--	2	3	--
Jack, Wm., & Math'w	1,200	6	4	13
Ireland, Hans	200	2	5	6
Irwin, Alex'r, single	--	--	--	--
Kirkpatrick, Ja's	--	1	1	4
Koontz, Philip	250	2	3	2

Hempfield Township	Acres	Horses	Cattle	Sheep
Kitsor, Philip	--	2	2	--
Kepple, Nich's	100	2	5	--
Kirk, James	--	1	--	--
Kimble, Jacob	150	2	3	2
Kifer, Henry	150	2	1	1
Kistor, Ludwick	--	2	2	1
King, James	150	2	3	2
Kaple, Jacob, single	--	--	--	--
Karr, Will'm	--	2	2	3
Larrimor, David	100	--	1	--
Love, Will'm	--	2	2	6
Long, Tobias	300	2	3	2
Lyon, Will'm	100	2	2	1
Litslone, Ab'm	--	1	2	--
Long, Nich's	--	1	--	--
Long, Ludwick	100	--	--	--
McInterfer, Dan'l	--	1	1	--
Moor, Jn'o, Esq'r	300	2	3	--
Moor, Ja's	300	2	2	--
Moor, Will'm	300	1	--	--
McKee, Hugh	50	1	1	--
McKee, James	300	6	3	9
McGwire, Jn'o	100	--	1	--
Myars, Adam	100	2	2	--
Millar, Chris'n	150	2	3	2
Millar, Math'w	--	2	2	--
McKee, Rob't	200	2	3	4
McConnell, Wm.	--	--	3	3
Mason, Tho's	300	3	3	--
Moor, Hugh, single	--	1	--	--
McKee, David, single	--	1	--	--
McKee, Marg't	200	--	--	--
Monysmith, Chris'r	--	2	1	--
McGregor, Collins	140	--	--	--
Muffley, John	--	1	2	--
Mire, Adam, Sen'r	200	2	3	3
Marchant, David	450	2	3	3
Marchant, Fred'k	160	2	2	1
Mecklin, Mich'l	200	1	1	2
Mecklin, Devalt, Jun'r	200	2	2	1
Mecklin, Devalt, Sen'r	200	4	5	6
Millirons, Philip	50	2	2	2
Millirons, Jacob	300	2	5	4
Mathias, Daniel	200	2	2	--
McMullen, Han'h	100	1	2	--
Millar, James	--	2	2	2
Mathias, George	100	2	1	--
Mire, Christ'n, single	--	--	--	--
McBrier, Nath'l	--	2	3	--
Mecklin, Jacob	300	3	4	6
Nalder, John	--	2	1	--
Nellson, Agness	150	--	1	--
Nellson, Wm., single	--	1	--	--
Neilly, Benj'n, single	--	1	--	--
Oury, Chris'r	150	2	2	--

Hempfield Township	Acres	Horses	Cattle	Sheep
Oury, Adam	150	2	2	--
Oliver, And'w	300	2	4	6
O'Nail, Cha's	--	2	2	--
Orr, Rob't	226	1	4	--
Otterman, Lud'k	150	2	5	6
Price, Thomas, single	--	--	--	--
Patty, George	260	2	2	--
Painter, John	--	2	3	6
Perry, Wm.	300	2	3	4
Painter, Geo.	250	3	4	2
Peck, Wm.	200	2	2	--
Perry, Jn'o	200	2	5	5
Pricker, Adam	--	1	--	--
Potter, Sam'l	150	2	3	1
Parks, Hugh	100	2	2	2
Painter, Jacob	100	1	2	--
Riddick, Jn'o	--	2	2	4
Rynn, Jn'o	300	--	--	--
Rice, Fred'k	150	2	2	--
Roup, Fran's	125	2	2	--
Rugh, Peter	190	3	4	4
Rugh, Cath'e	300	--	--	--
Rugh, Jacob	190	3	2	6
Rugh, Mich'l	--	1	2	--
Riddle, Wm.	--	2	2	2
Roistill, And'w	100	--	1	--
Rinn, Nich's	--	2	2	--
Stokeley, Tho's	--	--	--	--
Shields, John	500	4	6	12
Shafer, Adam	--	2	1	--
Selface, John	--	2	1	--
Smith, Philip	130	2	4	4
Sparr, Geo.	200	2	2	2
Smith, Shrist'r	--	1	2	4
Shrum, John	300	--	--	--
Straw, Jacob	300	3	3	4
Shelhamer, Peter	--	2	1	--
Smith, Mich'l	80	2	--	2
Shaw, Wm.	300	3	4	4
Shire, Nich's	--	2	2	--
Sype, Adam	150	--	--	--
Steward, Arch'd	50	2	2	--
Shotts, Mich'l	300	1	--	--
Shrader, Jacob	200	2	4	6
Sheak, Chris'n	--	2	1	1
Simpson, Tho's	300	2	3	2
Smith, Sam'l	50	1	1	--
Stott, Adam	100	1	2	--
Sheanor, Jacob	220	2	2	3
Smith, Geo.	50	1	1	--
Turner, Jn'o	600	4	2	--
Truby, Ch'r, Esq'r	150	3	4	5
Tanner, Geo.	300	3	9	12
Thomas, Garrard	300	4	9	12
Thomas, Wm.	300	--	--	--

Hempfield Township	Acres	Horses	Cattle	Sheep
Taylor, Rob't	200	1	1	3
Vandike, Wm.	100	1	1	5
Walker, Ja's	100	1	3	--
Waddle, Sam'l	--	2	2	2
Walter, Anth'y	400	2	2	4
Winsell, Jn'o	100	2	2	--
Waltenbaugh, Rineh'd	--	--	1	--
Willson, James	300	--	--	--
Welker, Mich'l	150	2	2	--
Williams, Tho's	300	2	2	7
Wiley, John	--	2	2	--
Weaver, John, single	--	--	--	--
Wilson, Edw'd	100	2	2	4
Waterson, Ja's	2	2	5	4
Weagly, Ab'm	200	--	--	--
Weagle, Isaac	100	2	1	1
Wilson, Cha's	--	2	2	4
Williams, Dan'l	250	3	4	3
Winymaker, Peter	200	2	2	3
Waltenbaugh, Tedor	--	2	1	--
Willson, Wm.	60	2	2	3
Walsh, Ja's	--	2	1	--
Walsh, Jn'o	150	2	2	1
Waugh, Jn'o	60	3	2	6
Wolf, And'w	--	2	2	--
Walter, Philip	--	2	1	--
Wesby, James	150	3	4	4
Wensell, Philip	100	1	--	--
Yokey, Ab'm	--	--	1	--
Young, Alex'r	150	2	2	1
Yount, Nich's	100	2	2	1

Huntington Township				
Adams, John	--	2	2	--
Alleot, Rob't	300	3	2	4
Andrews, Fra's	--	2	2	3
Alexander, Sam'l	--	2	2	3
Amberson, Jn'o	1,100	1	1	--
Armstrong, Wm. B.	--	--	1	--
Adams, Alex'r	--	1	2	--
Armstrong, Wm., single	--	1	2	--
Armstrong, Jn'o, d'o	--	1	--	--
Ardroy, Jn'o	200	1	1	--
Anderson, Wm., single	--	--	--	--
Baggs, Jn'o, d'o	--	--	--	--
Baird, Geo.	300	2	2	2
Blackburn, Jos'h	300	3	3	6
Baird, Wm.	100	2	2	3
Brannon, Geo.	300	1	1	--
Boall, Cha's	--	2	1	2
Brown, Benj'n	300	2	2	2

Huntington Township	Acres	Horses	Cattle	Sheep
Benson, Ja's	--	1	1	--
Baggs, Wm.	300	2	2	--
Baggs, And'w	--	1	1	--
Biarly, Jacob	--	2	1	--
Boyd, Tho's	--	2	3	2
Brown, Jn'o	--	1	2	--
Beaty, Wm.	400	2	3	4
Beaty, Jos'h	--	1	--	--
Brown, Rob't	50	3	3	4
Baggs, Math'w	150	2	1	2
Boall, Ja's, Sen'r	600	3	3	--
Boall, Henry	300	2	4	7
Boall, Ja's	300	2	2	3
Biarly, Mich'l	--	2	2	--
Berlin, Jacob	--	1	3	--
Barr, James	--	2	1	--
Beakem, Jn'o	300	1	2	4
Beasy, Jn'o	--	2	2	--
Buchannan, Wm.	300	2	2	--
Byars, And'w	300	2	1	--
Beacon, Wm.	--	1	1	3
Bell, Agness	--	2	--	--
Burns, Ja's	--	1	2	6
Boyd, Jn'o, W.	--	2	3	4
Boyd, Sam'l, single	--	1	--	--
Brodsword, Peter	150	2	2	3
Brodsword, Math's	--	2	2	4
Byram, Edw'd	--	2	2	--
Bealor, Jos'h	600	2	4	11
Buck, Jn'o	200	2	3	--
Bryney, Adam	150	1	2	--
Brewer, Mary	150	1	2	2
Brewer, Peter, single	--	2	--	--
Blackston, Ja's	300	4	4	22
Beer, Jn'o	250	2	3	4
Beer, Ja's	--	1	1	--
Boyd, Tho's	--	--	--	--
Blackburn, Jn'o	100	1	1	--
Blackburn, Jos'h, single	--	1	1	--
Buchannon, David	--	2	1	--
Becket, Rob't	100	2	3	3
Blackburn, Anth'y	200	3	4	17
Barr, Sam'l, single	--	--	--	--
Barr, Ja's, d'o	--	1	2	--
Blair, Jn'o, single	--	--	--	--
Cunningham, Henry	--	2	--	--
Creanor, Philip	100	2	2	--
Clark, Jn'o, single	--	1	--	--
Cochran, Jn'o, d'o	--	1	--	--
Cochran, And'w	300	--	--	--
Coulter, Ely	800	2	5	2
Cowan, Math's	300	2	2	--
Crutchlow, Wm., single	--	1	--	--
Cooper, Jn'o	60	2	2	3
Cristy, Jn'o	200	2	3	--

Huntington Township	Acres	Horses	Cattle	Sheep
Carson, Rich'd	560	2	1	--
Campbell, Pat'k	900	2	2	4
Carnahan, Ja's	300	4	4	8
Cristy, Jn'o	300	3	2	--
Calklazer, Ab'm	150	4	6	10
Cooper, Sam'l	--	1	1	--
Couz, Craft	--	--	--	--
Calklazer, Jn'o	300	4	5	2
Calklazer, David	200	1	1	2
Cowen, Dan'l, single	--	--	1	--
Cowen, Pat'k	40	1	1	--
Carnahan, Jn'o, Sen.	300	3	4	5
Carnahan, Jn'o, Jun'r	--	2	2	4
Carnahan, Jn'o	300	3	5	5
Caruthers, Ja's	50	2	3	3
Camp, Mathias	150	2	3	2
Camp, Garrard	150	3	3	6
Casady, Dan'l	--	2	3	2
Caldwell, Wm.	--	2	2	2
Caldwell, Alex'r	--	2	2	3
Caldwell, Rob't	--	2	2	--
Conrad, Jn'o	300	2	2	2
Coe, Ebenezer	--	2	2	4
Coe, Benj'n, Sen'r	--	2	2	1
Cummons, Jn'o	--	2	1	--
Campbell, Ja's	--	2	3	4
Coe, James	--	1	2	--
Campbell, Mich'l, single	150	2	2	--
Chambers, Ja's	--	2	2	--
Cristy, Ja's	--	2	1	2
Campbell, Jn'o	--	1	1	2
Caldwell, Math'w	--	3	1	--
Caldwell, Jos'h, single	--	1	--	--
Caldwell, Jos'h, Sen'r	200	3	6	10
Calwell, And'w, single	--	--	--	--
Cooper, Wm., single	--	--	--	--
Davison, John	100	2	3	6
Davis, John	150	2	2	--
Dier, John	--	3	2	2
Duncan, Ja's	100	3	3	2
Devoss, Joseph	150	2	1	--
Dill, Fran's	300	2	4	8
Dible, Jacob	--	3	4	3
Drain, Fran's, single	--	--	--	--
Davis, Wm.	--	2	2	4
Eckles, Chas	50	3	2	3
Eakin, Benj'n	--	1	2	--
English, James	--	2	2	--
Fulton, Ja's, single	250	2	2	3
Fry, Mich'l	200	2	1	--
Farran, Hugh	--	2	2	--
Fulton, Jn'o, Jun'r	150	3	4	11
Fulton, Wm.	150	2	3	4
Fitzgerald, Barth'w	--	1	3	8
Finley, And'w	300	2	2	3

Huntington Township	Acres	Horses	Cattle	Sheep
Reyburn, Adam	200	2	2	--
Rollins, Anth'y	--	2	2	--
Rudibaugh, Ad'm	600	2	3	4
Read, Rob't	300	1	2	--
Rea, James	--	2	2	--
Robinson, James	15	1	1	3
Rogers, Rob't	--	1	2	--
Rollins, James	--	3	2	2
Raney, Law'ce, single	--	1	--	--
Reed, Ja's	50	2	2	--
Roney, Pat'k	100	2	1	--
Ralph, Tho's	200	2	2	3
Ragan, Philip	53	2	1	--
Reardon, Jn'o	100	--	2	--
Reardon, Dennis	300	2	2	5
Robertson, Jn'o	300	3	3	5
Rulle, Sam'l	225	3	3	7
Rulle, Tho's	--	1	1	--
Ramsey, Ja's	--	--	1	--
Reynolds, Wm.	100	2	2	6
Rollins, Henry	200	1	1	--
Ross, Sam'l	--	1	1	--
Ross, Jn'o	300	2	6	4
Robertson, Ja's	300	3	3	4
Ralston, Wm.	200	2	3	3
Robertson, Tho's, single	250	2	1	--
Retherford, Jn'o	200	2	3	1
Richy, Edw'd, single	--	--	--	--
Sherry, Barny	200	1	--	--
Shannon, Jn'o	150	2	2	--
Scott, Wm.	--	2	1	--
Sturgeon, Sam'l, single	50	2	2	--
Summerville, Alex'r, S'r	300	2	2	4
Summerville, Alex'r, J'r	--	2	2	--
Stokely, Nch'h	800	3	6	7
Sams, Adam	250	3	3	7
Smith, Geo.	150	2	2	--
Shetler, Peter Coonrod	--	2	2	--
Studiberger, Peter	300	--	--	--
Studiberger, Ab'm	200	2	3	5
Studiberger, Jos'h	--	3	3	--
Smith, Jn'o, single	100	1	--	--
Sherer, Timothy	160	2	2	7
Steward, Wm.	100	2	2	--
Studiberger, Philip	--	1	--	--
Swift, Jn'o	50	1	1	--
Swan, Geo., single	300	1	4	--
Shaw, Ja's	300	2	2	--
Swab, Geo.	300	1	1	--
Stuot, Adam	--	2	2	--
Sanderson, Henry, single	--	1	--	--
Sample, David	300	4	5	3
Stimble, Isaac	--	1	1	--
Shillin, Geo.	500	2	2	7
Streaker, Elias	--	2	2	--

Huntington Township	Acres	Horses	Cattle	Sheep
Fulton, Ab'm, Jun'r	--	2	2	4
Fulton, Ab'm, Sen'r	300	4	1	2
Fulton, Rob't, single	--	1	2	--
Fulton, Henry, d'o	--	1	2	--
Fletcher, Tho's	300	4	4	5
Funk, Martain	--	3	3	--
Forster, James, single	--	1	--	--
Frick, Nich's	50	1	2	2
Frick, George, single	--	1	--	--
Fulton, James	--	3	3	8
Finley, Mich'l	64	2	1	--
Frick, Henry, single	--	--	--	--
Guffy, James	300	2	2	3
Gill, Hugh	100	2	2	--
Gilkey, Wm., single	--	2	--	--
Gordan, Jn'o, d'o	100	2	--	--
Garvin, Marvin	100	2	1	2
Glenn, John, single	--	1	--	--
Gordon, Robert	--	1	3	--
Gray, Ja's, wh't	--	1	2	--
Gibson, Levy	--	2	2	2
Giffy, Thomas	--	2	2	--
Gabon, Jn'o, single	--	--	--	--
Hamilton, Rob't	100	3	3	6
Haslep, Rob't	300	2	2	--
Hamilton, Ja's	1,300	1	2	5
Hutchison, Ja's	--	2	3	4
Hill, Fred'k, single	300	1	--	--
Hill, Peter	--	2	3	--
Hill, Gasper	--	1	1	--
Hindman, Rob't Peter	40	2	2	4
Hall, John	--	3	2	1
Huey, Wm.	250	2	3	5
Hogan, Gaian	--	2	1	--
Huffman, Henry	150	2	2	4
Hogan, John, single	--	1	--	--
Haggis, Sam'l	150	2	2	--
Hill, David	--	2	3	4
Hollis, Wm.	180	1	2	--
Hendrix, Ab'm	100	2	2	--
Habbage, And'w	200	--	--	--
Hays, Chris'r	300	6	8	10
Henderson, Jn'o, single	--	1	--	--
Hoplets, Mich'l	--	1	2	--
Handley, Sam'l	250	2	5	4
Harper, Rob't	--	1	1	--
Hall, Rob't, single	--	--	--	--
Henry, Jn'o	--	2	2	3
Harper, Tho's	--	1	1	--
Hutchison, Ja's	--	3	2	4
Hunter, Wm.	300	3	4	9
Hunter, Patrick, single	--	1	--	--
Hunter, Rob't, single	200	1	--	--
Ham, Coonrod	--	2	1	--
Irwin, Henry	--	2	2	--

Huntington Township	Acres	Horses	Cattle	Sheep
Johnston, Rich'd, single	--	1	--	--
Irwin, Jn'o	300	4	16	--
Jackson, Tho's, single	--	--	--	--
Johnson, Tho's	300	2	2	--
Johnson, James	200	3	3	8
Jones, Thomas	250	3	4	10
Johnston, Alex'r	--	2	2	3
Jones, Evan	300	2	2	2
Johnston, John	--	1	3	--
Johnston, Hugh	--	2	--	--
Jack, John	300	2	2	6
Johnston, James	--	1	1	--
Jackson, Rob't, single	--	1	--	--
Jolly, David, d'o	--	--	--	--
Kyle, Edw'd	--	--	1	--
Kyle, Jn'o	300	2	2	--
Kerr, Rob't, single	--	1	--	--
Knox, David	80	2	2	2
Kithcart, Ja's	100	1	1	--
Kerr, Wm., single	--	1	1	--
Kerr, Paul	--	1	1	--
Kirkpatrick, Alex'r	150	1	1	--
Kilgore, Patrick	--	1	1	--
Kerr, Geo.	--	3	3	--
Kemson, Jn'o	--	2	1	--
Kerr, Ja's	--	1	2	--
Kinkead, Ja's	200	3	1	2
Kelly, Math'w	100	2	2	6
Kirkpatrick, Tho's	150	2	5	6
Kirkpatrick, Jn'o, single	--	1	--	--
Kilfillen, Tho's, d'o	--	1	--	--
Killbright, Ja's	50	2	2	3
Keffer, Henry	--	1	1	3
Kelly, Tho's, single	--	--	--	--
Kirkpatrick, Joseph, single	--	1	--	--
Ker, James	--	2	2	2
Kirkpatrick, Geo.	--	1	2	--
Leech, Sam'l	200	3	3	7
Logan, David	--	3	3	--
Long, John	200	2	2	--
Loutzinhiser, Peter	200	2	2	4
Leech, James	--	1	1	--
Loutzinhiser, Jacob	200	2	3	--
Lavour, Barnard	--	1	--	--
Long, Wm.	--	2	1	--
Lewis, Ezekiel	--	1	1	--
Logan, Thomas	--	1	--	--
Light, Peter	480	2	3	4
Light, John	--	2	2	6
Light, Jack	--	1	--	--
Latimore, Geo.	300	3	4	6
Laughead, Joseph	50	2	2	4
Lindsey, Jn'o, single	--	1	--	--
Lindsey, Hezekiah	150	2	2	1
Latta, Wm.	300	3	4	7

Huntington Township   Acres Horses Cattle Sheep

Name	Acres	Horses	Cattle	Sheep
Lutes, Geo.	--	--	1	--
Latimore, John, single	--	--	--	--
Lutes, Philip, single	--	--	--	--
McCleland, Jn'o	200	2	2	--
McCann, Jn'o	--	1	1	--
Martain, Wm., single	--	1	--	--
McCann, Henry	100	2	2	--
McDonold, Jn'o	100	2	2	--
Marshall, William	300	3	3	4
Morton, Jn'o	--	1	2	3
McCullough, And'w	--	2	3	2
Millar, Silas	--	2	1	--
Millar, Isaac	300	1	1	--
McGrew, Alex'r	250	2	3	--
McGrew, Jn'o	200	2	1	--
McClure, Sam'l	100	2	2	1
Mitchell, Hugh	106	2	2	4
Malson, Nich's	90	1	1	--
Malson, Dan'l, single	--	1	--	--
McHenry, Malcam	250	2	4	--
Millar, Mich'l	120	2	1	2
Murphy, Jn'o	--	1	1	--
Musan, Jn'o	150	1	1	2
McCaw, Jn'o	150	1	1	3
McCaw, David	150	1	2	3
McDade, Hugh	300	1	1	--
Millar, Jn'o, Esq'r	250	3	4	4
Martin, Ja's	--	2	1	--
Morrow, Sam'l	--	2	3	--
Millar, Jn'o	60	2	2	4
McCleland, Jn'o	100	1	1	--
McClintic, Henry	200	3	2	4
McClintic, Sam'l, single	20	2	1	4
McAnulty, Jos'h	--	2	2	--
McLaughlin, Wm.	--	2	2	4
Mitchell, Cha's	106	3	53	2
McCord, Ja's, single	--	1	--	--
McHutchin, Alex'r	--	1	--	--
McHutchin, Ja's	--	2	2	2
Martin, Wm.	300	2	4	5
McMullen, Jn'o	100	2	3	--
Mellendor, David, single	--	1	--	--
Mellendor, Jn'o	300	2	2	1
Mellendor, Wm.	300	3	3	2
McCurdy, Ja's	--	2	3	--
Mason, Tho's, single	300	3	--	--
McMical, Sam'l	--	1	1	--
McGrury, Tho's	--	1	1	3
McCaslin, Ja's	--	1	--	--
Morehead, Sam'l	60	2	2	6
Moore, Wm.	--	2	1	--
McBride, Jn'o	--	1	1	--
McBride, Wm.	300	3	4	5
McConnell, Jn'o	--	2	2	3
McAnulty, Rich'd	300	2	1	2

Huntington Township	Acres	Horses	Cattle	Sheep
Mercial, Gasper	400	4	6	2
Millegen, Jn'o	--	1	2	3
Miller, Isaac	60	2	3	1
McHenry, Jos'h	--	3	2	4
McHenry, Kain	200	2	6	--
McKinny, Jn'o, single	--	--	--	--
Moore, Jn'o, d'o	--	--	--	--
McCurdy, Ja's	--	1	1	--
McNaugher, Hugh, single	--	--	--	--
Musan, Philip	100	1	2	--
McGrew, Wm.	700	3	4	7
McGrew, Simon	150	2	4	6
McCasky, Math'w	300	2	2	2
Mullen, Ja's	100	1	2	--
Mains, Rob't	200	2	2	--
McKee, Jn'o	900	3	6	5
McKee, David	300	--	--	--
McGrew, Ja's	--	1	1	--
Mann, Wm.	150	4	3	1
Mann, Tho's	--	2	3	--
Mann, Jn'o	300	1	2	5
Martin, Ja's	200	--	--	--
Millar, Ja's, single	--	1	--	--
Millar, Gideon	300	2	3	4
Mellon, Hugh	--	1	1	--
McLucas, Jn'o, single	--	1	--	--
McClary, Tho's	--	2	2	--
McComb, Ja's	--	2	2	--
Nicholas, Tho's, single	200	1	--	--
Neely, Jo's	--	2	2	2
Newell, Marg't	300	2	3	3
Naman, Harmon	--	2	2	6
Naman, Wm.	--	2	2	--
Nesbit, Jerem'b	30	2	1	--
Nesbit, Wm.	200	2	3	3
Newling, Paul	--	1	--	--
Newell, Hugh	200	2	4	8
Newell, Rob't	300	4	5	10
Newell, William	300	4	5	5
Neal, Jn'o	300	3	7	4
Nichols, Jn'o	300	--	--	--
Owens, Wm.	300	1	2	--
Osburn, Sam'l	--	2	2	1
O'Kain, Patrick	--	2	2	--
Osburn, Wm.	--	2	1	--
Osburn, Jn'o	--	1	1	--
Pendergrass, Garrard	300	2	2	2
Patterson, Fra's	--	1	2	--
Peoples, Ja's	600	2	6	6
Perry, Sam'l	250	1	2	2
Paul, Ja's	--	2	2	1
Pusey, Henry	300	2	1	--
Porter, David	40	2	1	--
Patterson, Jn'o	--	1	1	--
Patterson, Ja's	100	2	3	2

Huntington Township   Acres   Horses Cattle Sheep

Shields, Wm.	--	2	2	3
Smith, Geo., Wm.,	150	--	--	--
Smith, Ja's, Col'o	600	3	6	4
Shields, David, single	100	--	--	--
Smith, And'w	--	2	1	--
Snider, Peter	--	2	2	4
Shields, Sam;l	--	2	1	3
Swoop, Nich's	280	1	1	--
Stuart, James	--	1	2	6
Sample, Ezek'l, single	--	--	--	--
Shannon, Henry	--	1	1	--
Scott, Jn'o	300	2	2	--
Thompson, Jn'o	300	2	2	--
Taylor, Ab'm	350	1	3	--
Thompson, Sam'l	200	4	6	5
Thompson, Ja's	150	2	4	--
Todd, Sam'l	300	2	4	4
Tarrenger, Mich'l	--	1	2	--
Tarr, Jn'o	300	2	2	2
Tait, Sam'l	--	2	1	--
Thomson, Tho's	60	2	2	--
Threw, Adam	15	1	1	1
Thompson, Anth'y	300	1	2	--
Taylor, John	100	2	2	4
Thompson, James	150	--	--	--
Vanleer, Math'w	300	5	4	6
Vance, David	300	3	4	8
Veal, John	--	2	2	--
Vance, George	150	3	2	7
Vigal, Will'm	100	1	1	2
Vance, Wm.	--	1	2	4
Vigal, Philip, single	--	--	--	--
Wallace, Ja's	200	2	2	--
Walthour, Geo.	150	2	3	6
Whitehead, Val'e	150	3	5	6
Walthour, Chris'r	150	3	5	6
Walthour, Mich'l, single	300	1	--	--
Wilson, Tho's	--	2	2	--
Wiggain, Jn'o	100	2	2	--
Wilson, Jn'o	300	2	2	--
White, Agnes	300	2	3	7
Wauson, Cha's, single	20	1	1	1
Watson, Wm.	--	1	2	2
Warnack, Edw'd	--	2	1	--
Wauson, Ja's	100	2	2	--
Wells, Ja's	300	2	2	5
Wood, Jn'o	60	2	2	3
Weagley, Ab'm	--	1	2	--
Wallis, Tho's	--	2	2	--
Willson, Rob't	--	2	3	4
Willson, Robert, cooper	--	1	2	8
Wardin, Sam'l	200	2	4	7
Woodrow, Jn'o	200	2	2	6
Wilson, Sam'l	300	3	6	8
Williams, Dan'l	--	1	1	6

Huntington Township	Acres	Horses	Cattle	Sheep
Wilson, Ja's, single	300	3	2	--
Wyre, Wm.	--	1	1	--
Walker, Gedior, single	--	1	--	--

	Springhill Township			
	Acres	Horses	Cattle	Sheep
Ashcraft, Ichabud	30	4	13	8
Arrowsmith, Ja's	--	2	2	--
Archer, Anth'y	2	1	1	4
Anderson, Ja's	15	2	1	6
Abram, Enoch	40	2	3	7
Archer, Wm.	--	1	1	--
Ashcraft, Jn'o	20	2	6	5
Archer, John	5	1	1	4
Ashcraft, Amos	5	2	1	--
Averly, Leonard	11	1	1	--
Averly, Nich's	--	2	2	6
Ashcraft, Eph'm	--	2	2	--
Byers, Philip	--	2	1	3
Barrackman, Fred'k, single	--	--	--	--
Bradibury, Coonrad	--	1	2	6
Barkley, Jn'o, Sen'r	20	3	3	6
Barkely, Ja's, single, gone	--	--	--	--
Baker, Nich's	--	2	4	--
Bellenger, Rudy	25	4	3	3
Bowman, Philip	--	1	2	--
Burk, John	--	--	1	--
Blake, Nich's, single	25	1	--	--
Brown, Basil	--	2	2	6
Bacchus, Wm.	20	2	2	3
Bacchus, Cath'e	15	1	2	3
Bacchus, Peter	40	2	2	3
Bevelin, Jn'o	4	1	1	--
Baily, Silas	--	2	1	3
Bowers, Basil	30	2	6	11
Buchannon, Alex'r	20	2	4	10
Brumfield, Emson	45	4	6	3
Bridgwaters, Sam'l	--	2	--	--
Bowers, Thomas	25	2	5	6
Berry, Joseph, single	--	--	--	--
Bell, James, d'o, gone	--	--	--	--
Bell, Hump'y, d'o	--	--	--	--
Brumfield, Rob't	--	1	2	8
Burckham, Cath'e	15	1	--	--
Bonnett, Lewis	--	2	1	16
Berry, Sam'l	12	3	3	7
Black, Ja's	20	2	2	2
Bagle, Elias	--	1	2	--
Boyls, Wm., single	--	--	--	--
Barns, Ezekiel	--	--	1	--
Brown, Josh	--	1	2	2
Barns, Silvanus	--	--	1	--

Springhill Township	Acres	Horses	Cattle	Sheep
Baker, Philip	15	1	1	7
Barrackman, Jn'o	30	2	--	6
Bell, Hump'y, Sen'r	--	1	3	--
Butler, Rachel	--	1	2	--
Bell, Ja's, Sen'r	--	2	1	--
Brown, Stev'n	--	2	1	--
Berry, Tho's, Sen'r	2	2	1	--
Beck, Jerem'h	--	3	1	--
Berry, Tho's	20	2	1	9
Bell, Jn'o	--	1	1	2
Bales, Jesse	25	2	1	--
Battan, Jos'h	--	1	1	--
Battan, Tho's, Sen'r	35	2	6	5
Battan, Tho's	--	2	2	--
Barrat, Sam'l	--	1	2	--
Barkley, Jn'o, Jun'r	30	2	5	4
Bowin, Sam'l	9	2	2	--
Brooks, Jerem'h	--	--	2	--
Brown, Rob't, single, gone	--	--	--	--
Boyers, Philip	--	1	--	--
Coon, Anth'y	25	2	2	5
Clauson, Garrard, single, gone	--	--	--	--
Clare, Tho's, single	--	2	2	--
Caldwell, Jos'h	30	3	4	5
Churchill, Rich'd, single, gone	--	--	--	--
Conn, George	30	3	3	9
Cox, John	--	1	1	2
Cox, Joseph	--	2	2	1
Clover, Jacob	--	2	1	--
Catt, Jn'o	--	--	1	--
Cooper, Jn'o	--	1	1	5
Coon, Coonrad	--	1	1	--
Catt, George	30	2	2	--
Callahan, Wm.	8	2	1	1
Clark, Jerem'h	9	2	2	2
Cushman, Isaac	15	1	3	4
Cross, Wm.	15	2	2	--
Combs, Jos'h, Sen'r	40	4	4	8
Combs, Jesse	--	1	1	2
Combs, Joseph	--	2	1	--
Combs, Jon'a	--	2	1	--
Coon, Joseph	--	1	1	6
Collins, John	--	2	3	7
Campbell, Ja's	--	--	1	--
Calvin, Ja's	8	1	2	--
Carr, Elisha	--	2	1	1
Carr, Jn'o, Sen'r	30	2	3	4
Carr, Jn'o, single, gone	--	--	--	--
Carr, Tho's, single	20	1	--	--
Carr, Elijah	20	2	2	--
Carr, Moses	30	3	3	4
Colman, Chris'r	--	1	--	--
Croushour, Nich's	20	2	2	10
Caldwell, Elberton	--	1	2	--
Catt, Philip	--	2	2	--

Springhill Township	Acres	Horses	Cattle	Sheep
Catt, Mich'l	30	2	2	--
Christy, Mich'l	40	2	2	2
Cains, Dan'l	--	1	2	2
Cooper, Wm.	--	1	--	--
Davy, Jos'h	--	2	3	--
Davy, Thomas	--	1	2	--
Draggo, Peter	--	--	1	--
Duffey, Mich'l	30	3	2	3
Draggo, Baltzar	24	2	2	2
Draggo, Peter, Jun'r	6	--	2	--
Devall, Marg't	15	2	1	3
Davis, Philip	4	2	2	8
Davis, Sam'l, single	--	2	1	--
Dean, Rich'd	--	2	2	9
Davis, Owen	20	2	3	4
Davis, John	6	2	1	4
Dean, Benj'n	14	2	2	12
Dougharty, Ja's	30	4	3	1
Davis, Wm.	--	1	1	--
Dall, James	15	3	3	8
Donaldson, Susanah	--	--	1	--
Devall, Pierce, Jn'o	60	6	5	6
Devall, Notley, single, gone	--	--	--	--
Dillenger, Barbary	18	3	2	5
Dawson, Thomas, single, gone	--	--	--	--
Drake, John	40	2	7	5
Drago, Wm.	--	--	1	1
Dush, Geo., single, gone	--	--	--	--
Evans, Hugh	20	5	5	14
Everly, Adam	--	--	2	1
Edwards, Peter, single	--	--	--	--
Fansier, Wm.	--	2	2	--
Fink, Henry	--	2	4	--
Finley, Isaac	15	3	6	17
Finley, Rich'd	35	3	6	24
Flowers, Lombard	--	2	2	6
Foster, Agnus	5	1	2	2
Ferry, Hugh	--	--	1	--
Ferry, James	--	--	1	--
Franks, Mich'l, Sen.	10	2	3	--
Fink, Daniel	--	2	1	--
Facit, Thomas	4	2	2	--
Fleeharty, Ja's	16	2	1	6
Ferst, Jacob	20	2	1	6
Fraize, Wm.	--	--	--	5
Frirkney, Henry	--	1	1	--
Franks, Mich'l	40	2	2	4
Fleck, Wm.	--	1	1	--
Fast, Nich's	30	1	2	4
Fast, Fra's, single	--	1	--	--
Fast, Jacob	--	1	1	--
Franks, Jacob	30	3	2	10
Gray, Jerem'h	12	2	3	--
Gilkey, Wm.	--	1	2	2
Gray, Ja's	30	3	3	--

Springhill Township	Acres	Horses	Cattle	Sheep
Griffith, Jn'o	60	2	3	10
Gilkey, David	--	2	3	9
Glasgow, Jn'o	15	1	3	6
Goodwin, Jos'h	4	1	2	--
Goodwin, Benj'n	--	1	2	1
Gilmore, Math'w	10	--	1	--
Garrison, Leonard	--	2	2	--
Gibbons, Ja's	4	1	--	--
Graham, Jn'o	--	1	--	--
Grinstaff, Lewis	--	1	1	--
Gallaspy, Geo.	18	2	1	--
Goosman, Chris'r	--	2	--	--
Gilmore, Ja's	40	2	3	9
Glover, Uriah	--	2	3	9
Gather, Wm.	--	--	1	--
Griffin, Cha's	60	2	3	9
Howard, Charles	--	2	2	6
Hill, Wm.	10	1	1	2
Hanna, Eliz'h	--	1	--	2
Hanna, Rob't	--	2	1	--
Halsclay, Ja's	30	--	--	--
Hardin, Mark	70	10	--	--
Hudson, John	--	2	1	1
Hardin, Abr'm	--	1	2	--
Hardin, Jn'o, Maj'r	--	3	2	6
Hardin, Martin, single	50	2	1	3
Hardin, John, miller	30	8	4	28
Hardin, Steven	--	3	3	3
Hardin, Benj'n	150	4	4	12
Heady, Thomas	40	2	2	7
Hamilton, Jn'o, Sen'r	--	1	3	--
Hamilton, Jn'o, single	--	1	--	--
Hardin, Rob't	--	1	2	3
Hardin, Mary	--	1	1	--
Hume, John	17	3	4	17
Hendrix, Ab'm	6	1	2	1
Harrison, Rob't	30	3	3	5
Hawfield, Devalt	30	3	3	2
Hawfield, Peter	--	1	3	3
Hawfield, Mathias	20	2	3	3
Hawfield, Cath'e	30	--	3	3
Hogelin, Wm.	25	4	2	10
Hill, Wm., single, gone	--	--	--	--
Hallin, Tho's	--	2	1	10
Hill, Jn'o	25	1	1	--
Hill, Rob't, single	--	--	--	--
Heaton, Jn'o	20	2	3	6
Heady, Tho's, Sen'r	35	3	4	6
Huston, Rob't	--	2	2	1
Hughey, Ja's	20	4	6	14
Holloback, Geo.	--	1	1	--
Hardin, Eden	--	--	2	2
Hout, Eliz'a	--	2	2	--
Huckleberry, Fred'k	15	2	3	--
Hautt, Peter	--	2	2	4

Springhill Township	Acres	Horses	Cattle	Sheep
Harris, Jonathan	3	1	1	3
Hendrix, Simon	5	2	2	--
Hand, Levy, single, gone	--	--	--	--
Howard, James	--	--	1	2
Hardin, John	--	2	1	4
Hardin, Tho's, single, gone	--	--	--	--
Jones, Morgan	5	2	4	--
John, Thomas	12	2	2	5
John, David	15	1	3	3
Jinkins, Philip	20	2	3	4
Jinkins, Jn'o	20	2	2	1
Jolly, Nelson	--	2	2	2
Jinkins, Wm., single	--	1	--	--
Kinkead, Sam'l	28	2	2	8
Kidd, Dan'l	--	2	4	--
Kerroll, Anth'y	--	1	3	--
Kelly, Sam'l	10	1	2	--
Kelly, Tho's	--	1	2	5
King, Wm.	--	1	1	--
Kennison, Ja's	--	1	1	1
Kennison, Jn'o	30	3	3	6
Kennison, Jos'h	40	2	4	7
Kelly, Patrick	--	2	2	--
Lewis, Philip, Sen'r	--	1	1	--
Lukis, Robison	10	2	3	--
Lanom, Wm.	12	2	1	8
Lukis, Richard	25	2	4	8
Larsh, Charles	--	2	1	--
Larsh, Paul	50	3	3	12
Lewis, Philip	--	2	2	--
Lawrance, Philip	--	--	2	5
Levingston, Jn'o	--	1	1	--
Lindor, Simon	--	1	2	--
Laswell, Thomas	--	1	1	--
Lyon, John	--	1	1	2
Lesly, Thomas	9	--	2	2
Lesly, Jn'o, single, gone	--	--	--	--
Lesly, Wm., d'o	--	--	--	--
Lynch, Jn'o	--	2	3	1
Lukis, Jn'o, single	40	2	2	2
McMullen, James	2	3	4	2
McFarlain, Jn'o	25	3	3	8
Merrifield, Mary	--	--	2	--
Merrifield, Sam'l	--	--	1	--
Morgan, David	100	4	5	12
McFarson, Alex'r	--	1	1	--
Masterson, Sarah	25	1	2	4
Martain, Asa	--	1	2	4
Moore, Aaron	50	3	4	12
Mitchell, Nath'l	--	1	1	--
Mitchell, Wm.	95	3	4	--
Merrifield, Rich'd	--	1	1	--
McHaffaty, Alex'r, single, gone	--	--	--	--
McLaughlin, Tho's	--	1	1	--
Martain, Jn'o, Jun'r	9	1	2	4

Springhill Township	Acres	Horses	Cattle	Sheep
Martain, Jn'o	19	1	3	3
McLain, Rob't	30	4	3	5
Myer, Eliz'a	--	2	2	--
Myers, Fred'k	25	2	1	8
Myers, Adam	25	1	2	--
Mason, John	25	2	3	6
Mesor, Ab'm	--	2	2	2
Mason, Martain	15	2	3	2
Main, John	30	2	2	5
Main, Philip	--	1	--	--
Main, Geo.	--	1	--	--
Main, Henry	--	1	--	--
McClellan, Wm.	30	2	4	2
McCleland, Ja's, Sen'r	12	2	2	--
McCleland, Ja's	--	1	--	--
McPike, Dan'l	15	1	1	5
Moore, Ann	30	4	6	13
Moore, Sam'l, single, gone	--	--	--	--
Moore, Tho's	10	2	--	--
Moore, Rob't	2	1	1	--
McMullin, Ja's	10	2	2	3
McCreary, And'w	6	2	2	3
Minsor, Dan'l	12	2	2	--
McIntire, Elenor	--	3	3	1
Marshall, Hugh	--	2	2	2
Marshall, Ralph	--	--	1	--
McEdoo, Jn'o, single, gone	--	--	--	--
McDonold, Isaac	--	2	4	3
McDonold, Jn'o	40	4	3	2
McDonold, Da'd, single	--	2	--	--
McDonold, Alex'r	30	2	4	7
Moore, Ezekiel	25	3	4	9
Mason, Philip	15	2	3	--
Murry, Tho's	--	--	1	2
McIntire, Jn'o	--	1	1	--
Murphey, Wm.	--	--	1	--
McHafaty, Wm., single, gone	18	3	1	1
McHafaty, Adam, d'o	--	--	--	--
Notts, Solomon	--	2	2	--
Neel, James	30	3	4	6
Neel, Jos'h	24	2	2	4
Newman, Isaac	25	4	3	15
Newn, Chris'r	--	--	2	2
Nixon, Jona'n	30	3	2	--
Ocull, James	20	2	3	4
Peters, Godfrey	--	1	1	--
Pettyjon, Jn'o	14	1	2	--
Powell, Thomas	--	3	2	4
Pain, Sam'l	20	2	3	9
Philips, Theop's	60	4	8	12
Prather, Bas'l, single	--	3	--	--
Person, Jn'o	--	1	1	--
Philips, Jn'o	5	--	2	1
Province, Sarah	46	3	4	--
Paterson, Jn'o	--	1	--	--

Springhill Township	Acres	Horses	Cattle	Sheep
Parker, Sam'l	--	1	1	--
Prightbill, Jacob	--	1	1	--
Prighblil, Pet'r, single, gone	--	--	--	--
Poundstone, Rich'd	25	2	3	2
Piercehour, Geo.	--	1	1	--
Patton, Fra's &, Patton, Rob't, g.m. [g.m. is used as the abbreviation for grist mill. - compiler]	1	--	--	--
Patton, Fran's	--	2	2	--
Patton, Rob't	--	1	1	4
Philip, Thomas	--	2	3	6
Powell, Rich'd	--	2	2	6
Pough, Jacob	--	2	2	--
Pierce, Philip	40	3	5	15
Pock, Nich'ls	30	2	1	8
Pock, Mich'l	--	--	1	3
Phillips, Mary	--	--	2	--
Piles, Zach's, single, gone	--	--	--	--
Pittsor, Chris'r	40	2	4	5
Porringer, Sam'l	10	2	2	--
Pane, Jonath'n	--	1	2	--
Pricket, Josiah	--	2	4	6
Quordin, Adam, single, gone	--	--	--	--
Rubbill, Sam'l	3	--	--	--
Robins, Isaac	--	1	1	--
Rogers, Henry	--	2	1	5
Reas, Jonath'n	100	5	8	26
Robins, Rich'd	12	2	2	1
Robins, Dan'l	40	3	2	6
Rutter, Jn'o	15	2	3	6
Right, Henry	--	--	1	--
Rich, Jacob	35	2	4	6
Rifle, Mathias	--	1	--	--
Rifle, Jacob	40	2	4	8
Rifle, Nich's	--	2	2	4
Rhodes, Anth'y	4	2	3	4
Rogers, Tully	5	2	1	4
Richie, Rob't	45	1	4	6
Row, Jacob	--	1	1	1
Robertson, Henry	18	2	3	6
Robertson, Ja's, single	--	1	--	--
Rogers, Hannah	--	1	--	--
Rogers, Philip, Jun'r	40	1	2	4
Ross, Jn'o	20	4	6	7
Rogers, Philip, Esq.	50	4	2	--
Rogers, Jn'o	--	1	3	1
Reed, Thomas	--	1	2	6
Reed, Rich'd	14	3	2	6
Reed, Caleb	8	1	1	6
Rifle, Geo.	25	2	3	6
Russell, Tho's	--	1	1	--
Russell, Jn'o	--	2	1	8
Roberts, Phil., single, gone	--	--	--	--
Rowland, Evan	8	3	3	--
Robertson, Susan'h	--	4	3	15
Ramsey, Tho's	50	3	7	7

Springhill Township	Acres	Horses	Cattle	Sheep
Robins, Wm.	--	1	2	--
Rabb, And'w, Esq'r	6	1	2	6
Rogers, Jona'n, single	--	1	--	--
Sterling, Ja's	6	1	2	--
Swearingen, Jn'o, Sen'r	50	2	4	10
Swearingen, Van	10	3	2	--
Swearingen, Jn'o, Jun'r	20	2	3	11
Sutton, Ja's, Rev'd	30	2	2	14
Sutherfield, Benj'n	--	1	2	--
Shanks, Jn'o	--	2	1	--
Smiley, Wm.	8	2	1	2
Shaklett, Benj'n	15	2	1	3
Shaklett, Jn'o	20	2	3	6
Salsberry, Wm.	30	2	5	8
Stouk, Philip	12	2	3	11
Smith, Peter	--	2	1	--
Simpson, Gater	20	2	2	--
Simpson, Allen	12	3	2	--
Shins, Geo.	16	2	1	--
Shoemaker, Jn'o	--	2	1	--
Snodgrass, Cha's	--	3	4	8
Sholey, Adam	50	2	3	--
Shively, Chris'r	--	2	4	7
Stilts, Jn'o	12	4	3	9
Siers, Dav'd	40	--	--	--
Snider, Rudolph	--	2	4	9
Sankston, Isaac	21	3	2	3
Stillwell, Ann	15	1	3	5
Stevenson, Edw'd	4	2	2	--
Steward, Geo.	--	1	3	2
Scott, Jn'o	20	3	3	6
Stillwell, Obed'h	--	2	2	2
Stillwell, Jos'h	10	2	2	7
Shelby, David	12	2	5	15
Silkwood, Basil, single	--	--	--	--
Sutherday, Jacob, single	--	--	--	--
Smith, Wm.	--	3	2	3
Smith, Augustus, single	--	1	1	5
Smith, Henry	16	2	2	--
Smith, Amos	--	1	3	6
Sweadwink, Jn'o	--	1	2	--
Smith, Philly	--	1	--	--
Smith, Philip	50	3	4	6
Steel, James	--	2	2	5
Streadler, Jn'o	25	1	1	5
Switzar, Peter	--	2	1	2
Shively, Philip	--	1	2	6
Silsor, Jonath'n	20	2	2	2
Shively, Jn'o	35	2	5	7
Springer, Zedi'k	40	3	4	7
Silsor, Geo.	--	2	2	--
Sears, Dan'l	25	2	2	2
Shuttleworth, Tho's	19	2	2	1
Silsor, Jn'o	40	3	3	5
Stevens, Henry	--	2	2	1

Springhill Township	Acres	Horses	Cattle	Sheep
Snair, Mich'l	40	1	1	--
Smith, Jn'o, single	--	1	--	--
Stillwell, Jos'h, d'o, gone	--	--	--	--
Tobin, George	20	4	2	4
Thomas, Owen	40	3	2	6
Thomas, Aeneas	--	1	2	6
Thomas, Henry	--	2	1	3
Tucker, Geo.	--	1	1	--
Tucker, Jn'o, little	--	1	1	--
Tucker, Jn'o	--	1	1	--
Thomas, Jos'h	--	2	7	4
Tebalt, George	50	3	4	12
Tivebaugh, Coonrad	15	3	2	6
Thomas, Edw'd, single, gone	--	--	--	--
Tush, Cath'e	30	1	1	1
Thomas, Jn'o	--	1	2	--
Treux, Obed'h	--	2	4	5
Templeton, Ja's	--	--	2	--
Tucker, Sam'l	--	--	2	--
Whiteley, Cha's	12	2	3	12
Wells, Am.	3	2	3	7
Wells, Ab'm	35	2	1	6
Williams, Basil	--	2	2	--
Williams, Geo.	--	2	2	9
Williams, Elisha	--	1	1	--
Williams, Will'm	--	1	1	--
Williams, Geo., Sen'r	30	4	4	15
Wade, Alex'r	8	1	1	4
Wade, Mary	--	1	--	2
Walker, John	22	2	6	1
Watson, Wm.	--	1	3	9
Watkins, Evan	--	2	4	9
Winsor, James	--	1	1	5
Wilkinson, Jn'o	150	3	2	--
Wadman, Chris'r	20	2	1	3
Walters, Eph'm	25	4	3	12
Wisted, Humph'y, single, gone	--	--	--	--
Wells, Levy	50	2	3	6
White, Ja's	35	1	5	5
Walters, Coonrad	--	2	1	--
Wood, Dan'l	40	2	3	8
Waits, Jn'o	20	2	4	8
Waits, Rich'd	--	1	2	--
Waid, Wm.	--	2	1	4
Wetherington, Wm.	30	2	2	6
Wetherington, Mark	--	1	--	--
Wethington, Mary	--	1	1	--
Waid, George	--	2	3	4
Waid, Windman, single, gone	--	--	--	--
Waid, Tho's	20	2	1	7
Webb, Jn'o	3	2	2	2
Workman, Wm.	4	2	1	4
Waid, Jn'o, M.	8	1	1	2
Walker, Ja's	5	2	2	8
Wade, John	--	1	4	10

Springhill Township	Acres	Horses	Cattle	Sheep
York, Ezekial	--	2	2	4
York, Jesse	--	3	5	2
York, Joshua	--	1	2	5
Young, David	--	2	2	6
Yeager, Joseph	35	1	3	8
Yeager, George	--	1	2	3
York, Jerem'h	--	1	1	--

Mount Pleasant Township

	Acres	Horses	Cattle	Sheep
Arnold, Jn'o	119	2	2	2
Anderson, Wm.	200	3	3	3
Allison, Moses	100	1	2	2
Aker, Simon	300	--	--	--
Amelong, Chris'r	100	2	1	--
Arnold, Dan'l	20	1	1	1
Alexander, Nath'l, single	--	--	--	--
Bealor, Jos'h	--	1	--	--
Bays, David	--	1	2	--
Bradley, Sam'l	300	3	3	--
Brumfield, Ja's	--	1	1	--
Bradley, Jn'o	50	2	1	--
Briney, Jn'o	150	1	2	3
Branker, Henry	600	3	2	--
Bays, Hugh	300	1	1	2
Byars, Coonrod	350	1	2	3
Bash, Martin	50	2	3	4
Bryan, Wm.	100	1	1	--
Black, Ja's	200	--	--	--
Blane, Eph'm	300	--	--	--
Barny, And'w	300	1	2	2
Bear, Rudy	150	2	3	7
Bear, Henry	100	2	2	2
Bole, Ja's	--	1	1	--
Brown, Ja's	--	1	1	--
Bell, Rob't	--	1	2	--
Bell, Wm., single	--	1	--	--
Bear, Adam, single	--	1	--	--
Boyd, Tho's, Sen'r, d'o	--	1	--	--
Brown, Wm., single	--	--	--	--
Butler, Tho's, d'o	--	--	--	--
Bays, Wm.	--	1	--	--
Bear, Rudolph	--	2	2	--
Barr, Rob't	--	2	2	--
Baird, Jn'o, Esq'r	100	2	2	4
Campbell, Cha's	200	2	4	3
Cherry, Ralph	700	4	5	--
Clark, Ja's	100	2	2	--
Carver, Jacob	110	1	2	2
Campbell, Geo.	200	2	2	--
Carter, Barziila	100	2	2	1

Mount Pleasant Township	Acres	Horses	Cattle	Sheep
Callan, Patrick	--	1	1	--
Clipener, Geo.	--	1	1	--
Chambers, Moses	--	1	1	--
Crawford, Ja's, single	100	2	2	4
Crawford, Geo.	100	2	2	4
Couze, Philip	20	2	2	4
Clark, Ja's, Cap'n	300	4	4	10
Crawford, Jn'o	100	2	2	3
Campbell, Jos'h	200	3	3	7
Colemer, Coonrod	200	2	1	--
Coulter, Sam'l	130	2	3	4
Cochran, Rob't	100	2	3	4
Cane, Martha	300	2	2	4
Craig, Jn'o, Cap.	50	3	2	--
Craig, Alex'r, Cap., single	150	1	--	--
Courtney, Eliz'a	200	1	2	2
Clinglesmith, Jacob	200	2	2	--
Crow, James	--	1	1	--
Campbell, Jn'o	--	1	2	2
Clark, Wm.	--	1	1	--
Cline, Jacob	--	2	1	--
Crow, Jn'o	--	1	1	--
Caswell, Sam'l, single	--	--	--	--
Crawford, Rob't, d'o	--	1	--	--
Clark, Jos'h	--	1	1	--
Consly, Peter	--	1	1	--
Dilforth, Widow	300	2	1	--
Divis, Elias	300	--	--	--
Donahoo, Jn'o	--	2	2	1
Dedman, Henry, single	--	--	--	--
Dilworth, Benj'n, d'o	--	--	--	--
Downing, Wm., d'o	--	--	--	--
Donahoo, Wm., d'o	--	--	--	--
Dunseth, Ja's, d'o	--	1	--	--
Dennison, Jn'o	--	3	2	--
Dilworth, Jn'o	--	2	1	2
Downing, Jn'o	--	1	1	--
Eager, John	150	2	1	--
Eager, Jos'h	150	3	2	--
Elliot, Tho's	150	3	1	3
Ekin, Wm.	200	2	2	--
Eager, Wm.	--	1	1	--
Elder, David, single	--	--	--	--
Eakin, James, d'o	--	--	--	--
Espy, Jacob	--	1	2	2
Fiskis, Garard	200	1	2	2
Fiskis, Jn'o	110	1	1	--
Finley, Wm.	250	2	5	6
Fletcher, Tho's	150	2	3	8
Farguson, Ja's	200	1	3	3
Fiskis, Ab'm	--	1	2	--
Frame, Jacob	--	2	1	2
France, Henry, single	--	--	--	--
Fisher, Adam	--	2	1	--
Fiskis, Cha's	100	1	1	--

Mount Pleasant Township	Acres	Horses	Cattle	Sheep
Guthrie, Jn'o, Esq'r	--	1	2	--
Guthrie, Ja's	100	2	2	--
Glenn, Ja's	100	1	2	--
Giffin, Jn'o	300	3	3	8
Garvin, Jos'h	--	2	2	--
Greer, Wm.	300	2	3	6
Guthrie, Ja's, Sen'r	210	2	2	--
Graham, Wm.	300	--	--	--
Gorely, Jn'o	--	2	2	2
Guy, James	--	1	2	--
Guthry, Jn'o, Jun'r, single	--	1	--	--
Guthrie, Wm., Cap., single	--	--	--	--
Gaff, James, single	--	--	--	--
Gordon, James	--	2	2	2
Galbreath, Jn'o	--	2	1	--
Hurst, Nath'l	610	7	7	12
Hunter, John	95	2	1	--
Henry, Geo.	300	2	4	3
Hopkins, Jn'o	--	--	--	--
Hutchison, Jn'o	100	2	4	3
Hunter, Ja's	300	2	4	10
Hurst, Henry	--	3	3	6
Herington, Barth'w	--	1	1	--
Hartley, Rob't, single	150	1	--	--
Hurst, Wm., d'o	--	--	--	--
Hare, Mich'l, d'o	--	--	--	--
Hopkins, Jos'h	--	1	2	4
Harring, Coonrad	--	1	2	--
Inman, Wm.	40	1	--	--
Jack, Jn'o	200	3	3	4
Jamison, Rob't	200	2	3	--
Jack, Patrick	100	2	2	2
Jamison, Jn'o	150	1	2	--
Johnston, Cha's	110	3	3	9
Jinkins, Wm.	100	--	--	--
Johnston, Ja's	100	--	--	--
Jarvis, Rich'd	--	1	1	2
Jamison, Jn'o, Sen'r	--	2	1	--
Inman, Henry, single	--	1	--	--
Jemmison, Marmaduke, single	--	1	--	--
Jemmison, Fran's	--	--	2	--
Jones, Tho's	--	2	2	2
Kerr, Rob't	--	2	2	--
Kirkpatrick, Wm.	100	2	1	--
Kilgore, David	250	2	3	6
Kilgore, Jn'o	200	--	--	--
Kinkead, And'w	--	1	2	2
Kays, Rob't, single	--	--	--	--
Little, Jacob	--	2	2	--
Lovenguire, Chris'r	500	3	4	10
Lavour, Chris'n	100	2	3	4
Latta, Moses	233	3	5	7
Lewis, Sam'l	200	2	2	3
Lazier, Ab'm	300	3	3	2
Lochry, Mary	150	1	2	2

Mount Pleasant Township	Acres	Horses	Cattle	Sheep
Lochry, Jerem'h	200	1	--	--
Lochry, Wm.	200	3	3	4
Lowers, Rob't	200	2	3	2
Lidick, Jacob	--	2	2	--
Lidick, Jn'o	--	1	2	6
Lazier, Dan'l	--	1	1	--
Lazier, Jn'o	--	1	1	--
Lewis, Sam'l, Jun'r, single	--	--	--	--
Lavour, Henry, d'o	--	--	--	--
John, Latta, d'o	--	2	--	--
Lavour, Barth'w	100	2	2	2
Lattimore, Wm.	--	1	1	1
McCibbin, Jn'o	200	2	2	--
McCleland, Jn'o	300	2	3	6
McMasters, Wm.	150	2	3	4
Martin, Hugh, Esq'r	160	3	5	--
McClure, Jn'o	200	2	2	2
McCall, Barn's	200	2	3	2
McMasters, Ja's	300	2	3	--
McCoy, Tho's	300	2	2	6
Morrison, Dan'l	150	2	2	--
McClenehan, Tho's	95	2	2	--
McKinny, Alex'r	100	2	2	2
Marshall, Rob't	100	2	2	3
McKee, Jn'o	130	1	2	4
McMullen, Rob't	210	3	2	6
Morrison, Math'w	40	2	2	4
Mitchell, And'w	100	1	2	2
McDonold, Geo.	200	2	1	--
Marshall, Ja's	200	2	3	--
McCleland, Geo.	100	1	2	2
McGinnis, Fra's	300	2	3	6
Moore, Jn'o	200	1	1	6
Maxwell, Wm., single	300	2	2	--
McCracken, Jn'o	50	--	--	--
McBride, Ja's	--	1	2	--
McKnight, Wm.	50	2	2	2
McKenny, Isaac	150	2	4	2
McGeary, Wm.	300	3	4	3
McGeary, Rachel	200	1	--	--
McWhister, Wm.	--	2	1	--
McFarlain, Walter, single	--	--	--	--
McDonold, Jn'o, d'o	--	1	--	--
McKee, Jame's, d'o	--	1	--	--
Murry, Neal, d'o	--	1	1	1
McKinny, Hugh, single	--	1	--	--
McClannahan, Ja's, d'o	--	--	--	--
McClanahan, Jn'o, d'o	--	1	--	--
Millegan, Wm., d'o	--	--	--	--
McGugin, Alex'r, d'o	--	1	--	--
Marshall, Ja's, d'o	--	1	--	--
Marshall, Archibald, d'o	--	1	--	--
Marshall, Ja's	--	2	2	8
Moore, Geo., single	--	--	--	--
McKissick, Isaac, d'o	--	1	--	--

Mount Pleasant Township	Acres	Horses	Cattle	Sheep
Mitchell, Ja's, d'o	--	1	--	--
Maxwell, Adam, d'o	--	1	--	--
Maxwell, Wm., d'o	--	1	--	--
McGwire, Wm.	--	2	2	--
McCleland, Ja's	--	2	3	--
Mcriland, Jn'o, single	--	1	--	--
McQuilkin, Ja's	--	1	1	--
Meek, Jn'o	--	2	2	--
Murphy, Jn'o	--	2	2	--
McCleland, Alex'r	--	1	2	2
McFarlain, Wm.	--	2	2	--
McLain, Paul	--	1	1	--
McCartney, Geo.	150	2	2	2
Marshall, James, single	--	1	--	--
Marshall, Wm.	--	2	1	2
McQueston, Ja's	200	1	3	1
Newell, Rob't	200	2	3	2
Neilly, Hugh	100	2	3	1
Nichols, Jn'o	300	5	8	--
Neal, Wm.	200	3	2	--
Newell, Josh'a	100	2	2	4
Nichols, Wm.	200	2	2	5
Nichols, Rob't	200	2	3	4
Neal, John	--	1	2	--
Newell, Jn'o, single	--	--	--	--
Newell, Ja's, d'o	--	--	--	--
Nichols, Jn'o, single	--	1	--	--
O'Harra, Arthur	150	3	2	6
Oakerman, Stophel, single	--	--	--	--
Peoples, Sam'l	200	2	4	6
Powers, Ja's, Rev'd	200	3	3	12
Palmer, Adam	100	1	2	2
Patton, Tho's	100	2	2	2
Powers, Jacob	50	2	3	2
Powers, Ab'm	150	2	5	5
Pershon, Chris'n	100	2	1	--
Pershon, Fred'k	100	4	4	8
Proctor, Jn'o	300	4	4	8
Proctor, Wm.	200	--	--	--
Peoples, Jn'o	200	2	3	3
Pollock, Ja's	20	2	2	--
Partmiser, Adam	200	1	2	--
Quin, Jn'o	100	2	2	--
Quigley, Cary, single	--	--	--	--
Riddle, Jn'o, single	--	1	--	--
Robertson, Jn'o, single	--	--	--	--
Rograld, Ja's, d'o	--	--	--	--
Robertson, Sam'l, single	--	1	--	--
Robertson, Wm., d'o	--	1	1	--
Ralston, Jn'o, single	--	--	--	--
Ray, Jos'h	100	2	1	--
Reynolds, Jos'a	200	4	5	12
Robinson, Wm.	300	4	4	3
Rowley, Jn'o	100	2	2	2
Robertson, Marg't	100	1	2	4

Mount Pleasant Township	Acres	Horses	Cattle	Sheep
Rugh, Anth'y	275	3	4	3
Robinson, Rob't	--	2	2	--
Raynor, Stophel	100	1	2	3
Rankin, David	300	2	3	7
Reasor, Fred'k	--	1	1	--
Robinson, Wm., single	--	1	--	--
Robinson, Rob't	150	3	4	1
Robinson, Hugh	--	1	1	2
Reileigh, Cha's	--	1	1	--
Ralston, Rob't	--	--	--	--
Rufinder, Simon	--	1	--	--
Robinson, And'w, single	--	--	--	--
Ryan, Geo.	--	2	1	--
Russell, Ja's	--	2	2	2
Shaltzberger, Henry	--	2	2	1
Speelman, Jn'o	100	1	2	--
Stockberger, Mathias	100	2	2	4
Shrader, Wm.	--	2	2	--
Steer, Jacob	50	1	1	--
Smitley, Gasper	100	--	1	--
Smitley, Gasper, Jun'r	100	2	2	--
Smitley, Nich's	60	2	1	1
Stockberger, Mich'l	80	2	1	--
Shearer, David	100	2	2	2
Smith, Philip	119	2	1	3
Sees, Chris'r	50	2	1	3
Selders, Geo.	100	2	1	--
Shepard, Jn'o	200	2	2	--
Syphritz, Bostion	100	2	1	3
St. Clair, General	500	--	--	--
Sorrels, Sam'l	100	2	4	6
Steward, Wm.	50	1	1	--
Steward, Jn'o	--	2	1	1
Simpson, Ja's	--	1	1	--
Scott, Ja's	20	--	2	1
Sloan, Sam'l	5	--	--	--
Sloan, Jn'o	150	2	3	--
Sloan, Wm.	150	2	4	6
Stutstill, Jn'o	90	2	2	4
Shepherd, Jn'o, single	--	--	--	--
Simpson, Tho's, single	--	1	--	--
Shrader, Aaron, d'o	--	--	--	--
Steer, Barnard, d'o	--	--	--	--
Scott, Knight, d'o	--	--	--	--
Sloan, David, d'o	--	--	--	--
Sloan, Sam'l, Jun'r, single	--	--	--	--
Scott, Jos'h	--	1	2	--
Simpson, Ja's	--	2	2	--
Simpson, Math'w	--	3	5	2
Shrader, Wm., Sen'r	300	3	3	6
Seynor, Mich'l	--	2	2	--
Stevenson, Wm.	--	--	2	--
Smith, Tho's	--	2	2	3
Still, Ja's	100	1	1	4
Smith, Rob't	150	--	--	--

Mount Pleasant Township	Acres	Horses	Cattle	Sheep
Thompson, Jos'h	300	2	3	2
Thompson, Wm., ridge	100	2	2	--
Thompson, Jos'h	50	2	1	--
Todd, Wm.	160	3	5	2
Tittle, Peter	300	2	3	6
Taylor, Jn'o	200	3	3	4
Toppins, Rob't	200	2	3	4
Thorn, Jn'o	150	2	2	2
Trimble, Jn'o, single	--	--	--	--
Trimble, Arch'd	--	2	2	1
Thompson, Wm.	--	1	2	3
Tanner, Ja's	--	2	2	3
Teamor, Adam	--	1	1	--
Todd, Sam'l	--	2	3	7
Taylor, Jn'o	200	2	3	5
Thom, Jn'o, single	--	--	--	--
Tomling, Zedic	--	--	1	--
Taylor, Will'm	--	--	--	--
Trimble, Tho's	--	--	--	--
Vance, Rob't	30	2	4	1
White, David	200	2	2	5
Worthington, Rob't	200	2	3	6
Wilson, Sam'l, single	200	2	2	--
Wilford, Jn'o	150	2	2	4
White, Arch'd	200	2	2	--
Walter, Jacob	50	1	1	3
Wiley, Jn'o	300	2	2	4
Whitesides, Sam'l	200	2	2	2
Watson, Widow	260	3	7	7
Waddle, Robert	150	1	2	2
Weaver, Adam	100	2	2	3
Weaver, Gasper	140	1	3	--
Winter, Thomas	--	1	1	--
White, And'w	--	1	2	1
Weasner, Jn'o	--	--	--	--
Wolf, Jacob	--	1	1	2
Waddle, Ja's	--	2	1	--
Wagnor, tory	--	1	1	--
Walker, Alex'r	--	2	3	4
White, Pat'k	--	1	1	--
White, Jn'o	--	1	2	--
Wade, Jn'o	--	2	1	--
Wingfield, Henry	--	1	1	--
Wilson, Hugh	--	2	2	3
Worthington, Ja's	--	1	3	--
Waltingbaugh, Tedor	--	1	1	--
Worthington, Wm.	--	1	1	--
Wilson, Sam., Carol'a [Carolina?. Ed.]	--	1	--	--
Worthington, Jacob	--	1	--	--
Waddle, Wm.	--	1	--	--
White, James, single	200	1	--	--
White, Jn'o, d'o	--	--	--	--
Young, Coonrod	--	1	1	--
Youghy, Chris'r	--	2	2	5
Youghy, Chris'r, Jun'r	--	--	1	2

Mount Pleasant Township	Acres	Horses	Cattle	Sheep
Yearin, Geo.	270	2	4	4
Youghy, Peter, single	--	--	--	--

Armstrong Township

Names - No. of Tracts.
Rev'd Mr. Smith 2
John Moor 1
And'w Stewart 1
Sam'l Waddle 1
----- Brown 1
And'w Wolf 1
Rob't Lowers 1
James Sorrels 1
John Wells 1
And'w Adams 1
Alex'r Fails 1
Ja's Campbell 2
Jn'o McCrady 1
Tho's Wilkins 1
Fred'k Rorer 1
Jn'o Donahoo 1
Geo. Hutabaugh 1
Cha's Campbell 3
Jn'o Cox 1
Alex'r McKee 1
Mich'l Sambel 1
Wm. Steward 2
----- Ramsey 1
John Downey 1
----- Altman 2
Joshua Elder 4
Tho's Roberts 1
James Brownfield 1
John Crips 1
Benj'n Armstrong 5
John Hart 1
----- Chain 1
Cha's Hardin 1
Jolly Rogers 1
Wm. Mount 1
Jn'o Smith 1
Widow Farguson 1
Wm. Robison 1
John Rutherford 1
----- Brown 1
Reynolds Laughlin 1
Wm. Smith 1
Wm. Hill 1
Ja's Gorden 1
Levy Gibson 1
Jn'o Gibson 1
Wm. McNeal 2
Widow Hilands 1

Names - No. of Tracts.
Joseph Dixon 2
Wm. Moore 1
Sam'l Dixon 3
And'w Walker 1
Tho's McCoy 1
----- Wiley 1
Jn'o McCleland 1
Ja's McFarlin 1
Ja's Huston 1
Sam'l Todd 1
Wm. Davis 1
Tho's Gibson 1
Widow Evans 1
Cha's Campbell 1
Ja's Simpson 1
Tho's Simpson 1
Wm. McKee 1
Widow Simpson 1
Geo. Dixon 1
Wm. Anderson 1
Moses Chambers 1
David Russel 1
Tho's McClanahan 2
Tho's Patton 1
Sam'l Kile 1
Widow Jeanes 1
Ja's Kelly 1
Jn'o Hutchison 1
Hugh Scott 2
Wm. Brown 1
Wm. Curry 1
Jn'o Bailey 1
Wm. Howard 1
Ja's Thompson 1
Forgy Morhead 1
Tho's Campbell 1
James Camble 1
Ja's McLain 2
Ja's Lemon 1
Wm. Lowrey 1
Arch'd Lemon 1
James Wilkins 3
Sam'l Moorhead 1
Geo. Trimble 1
Jos'h Scott 1
Ja's Ramsey 1
Jn'o Lidick 1
Stophel Rynor 1

Armstrong Township

Names - No. of Tracts.	Name - No. of Tracts.
Ja's Simral 1	Jn'o Kelly 1
James Reynolds 1	Wm. Espy 1
Wm. Taylor 1	Wm. Read 1
Jos'h Hopkins 1	Joseph Wilson 1
David Cummins 1	Dan'l McKissick 1
Jn'o Henry 1	Jn'o Hutchison 1
Jn'o Dailey 1	David Shields 1
Widow McCrea 1	Reynolds Laughlin 1
Alex'r Morehead 1	Alex'r Young 1
Cha's McGuire 1	Widow Simpson 1
Tho's McCrea 1	Jacob Macklin 1
James Hutchison 1	Rob't Elder 2
James Ramsey 2	Wm. Lemon 1
Rob't Willson 1	Wm. Watson 1
Jn'o Mathews 1	Hugh Neilly 1
Jn'o Mitchell 1	James Hughs 1
Ja's McLain 1	John Farran 1
Wm. McIntire 1	James Calhoon 1
Jo's Mitchell 1	Sam'l Evans 1
Sam'l Kilpatrick 1	Wm. Smith 1
Jn'o Flemming 1	Sam'l Finley 1
Jn'o Ewing 1	Benj'n Jacobs 5
Widow Thompson 1	Rich'd Wallace 1
Rob't Millar 1	Isaac Anderson 2
Ezekiel Mathews 1	Jn'o Jeffries 1
David Rankin 1	Humphrey Fullerton 5
Nich's Coleman 1	John Woods 1
Hugh Wilson 1	Wm. McCune 1
Jn'o Lasley 1	James Cooper 1
Jn'o Marshall 1	John Hagan 1
James Marshall 1	Rob't Gibb 1
Ab'm Fulton 1	Rob't Rogers 1
Rob't Harper 1	Wm. Bracken 3
Rob't Elder 3	Jn'o McMahon 2
Jn'o Beer 1	Edw'd Kelly 2
Tho's Campbell 2	Thomas Burd 3
Jn'o McGomery 5	Mich'l Hufnagle 1
Tho's Wilson 1	Macklin Devalt 1
Fred'k Rorer 1	John Smith 1
Wm. Anderson 1	Sam'l McCollough 1
Sam'l Sloan 1	

Fairfield Township

	Acres	Horses	Cattle	Sheep
General St. Clair	550	--	--	--
Tho's Galbraith	1,200	3	6	--
Jn'o Hamlee	300	--	--	--
Peter Snider	196	2	2	--
Robert Reed	300	--	--	--
John Reed	300	--	--	--
George Rowe	200	2	2	--
Rob't McDowel	--	1	2	--
Tho's Sutton	200	2	2	4
George Sutton	--	2	3	2
Dan'l Lavere	100	1	1	--
Wm. Jamison	100	--	--	--
Widow Jamison	--	1	1	--
Henry Hise	250	4	3	3
Rob't McDowel, Sen'r	--	1	1	--
Charles Clifford	200	3	2	--
John Smith	300	3	3	--
John Taylor	300	1	4	1
Peter Maharge	200	2	2	--
Will'm Piper	200	2	2	4
John McMillen	200	--	--	--
Widow McManus	--	2	2	--
John McCrackin	200	--	--	--

Name - No. of Tracts.
Richardson's orphans 1
Hump'y Fullerton 1
John McMullin 1
Dan'l McCoy 1
Mich'l Huffnagle 2
Henry Hartman 1
David Kilgore 1
Jos'h Whiteside 1
Jn'o Wilson 1
Dan'l Laney 1
Edw'd Halferty 1
unknown Name 1
Amos Stevens 1
Fred'k Nagle 1
Dan'l Hendrix 1
Ab'm Hendrix 1
Dan'l Carmical 1
Nich's Lute 1
James Pollock 1
Charles Griffin 1
John Hanna 1
John Minochre 1
Sam'l Finley 1
Rob't Knox 1
James McCurdy 1
And'w Brown's orphans 1
James Guy 1
Sam'l McMulin 1
Philip Freeman 1

Name - No. of Tracts.
Rev'd Mr. Henderson 1
Henry Hawk 1
Rob't Fleck 1
----- Hall 1
James Fleck 1
Alex'r Negley 1
Mich'l Cofman 1
Wm. Kilpatrick 1
James McCurdy 1
Absalam Hendrix 1
Tho's Burd 1
And'w Sharp 1
Sam'l Moorhead 1
And'w Robison 1
John Palmer 1
Tho's Miles 1
Will'm Esseck 1
John Barr 1
James Ramsey 1
David Taitt 3
John Peters 1
Sam'l Smith 1
Alex'r Johnston 1
Rob't Hanna 1
Hugh Porter 1
----- Bullock 2
John Cummins 1
James Brown 1

Donnegal Township	Acres	Horses	Cattle
Moses Allison	150	2	3
Patrick Archibold	200	2	2
Ab'm Bowers	100	2	4
Locwic Bunts	100	3	3
Jn'o Brand	100	3	3
Philip Byars	100	1	1
Jn'o Buck	50	2	1
Precilla Carter	150	3	2
Philip Dumbal	100	--	3
Peter Dumbal	220	3	3
Ab'm Dumbal	200	2	2
Geo. Eaker	200	2	3
Abel Fisher	150	2	3
Mich'l Hay	100	3	3
Geo. Huber	550	1	2
Jos'h Hufhans	220	2	2
George Hutchison	50	1	1
Henry Hook	--	2	1
Isaac Jones	20	1	--
Amos Jones	50	1	--
Geo. Kells	200	4	3
Mich'l Kolfman	--	1	1
Mathias Kern	200	2	1
Wm. Kern	40	1	1
Rob't Krofford	--	2	1
Nich's Lute	200	2	3
Stop'l Losset	50	1	2
Jn'o Millar	300	2	2
Jn'o Martin	200	2	1
Henry Marshall	100	2	1
Ja's Montgomery	200	2	--
Wm. McKints	150	1	2
Dan'l Moore	--	2	3
Rob't McDowel	100	2	1
Edw'd McDowel	100	2	1
Wm. Molvin	100	2	1
----- McCasky	50	--	--
Jn'o McLain	--	1	--
Adam Nesley	200	3	3
Martin Overly	300	2	2
Bastion Overly	80	2	1
Jn'o Purder	600	2	--
Eliezer Perkins	80	1	1
John Reed	--	2	2
Jn'o Robison	--	--	--
Jos'h Segorine	100	1	2
Sam'l Shannon	80	3	4
Rich'd Shannon	--	--	1
Benj'n Sutton	--	1	1
Lodwic Sheek	50	1	1
Gasper Senf	35	2	1
Jacob Sharow	150	3	3
Peter Shigley	--	--	--
Henry Scattob	300	5	4
Henry Olrey	200	3	3

Donnegal Township   Acres   Horses   Cattle

Henry, Jun'r Olrey   50   2   1
Rich'd Williams   278   4   4
Geo. Orr   50   2   1
John, single Brand   --   --   --
Wm., d'o McDowell   --   --   --
Eleazar, d'o Porekins   --   --   --

                    Inhabitants of Manallen Township

Allen, Hugh   Burgh, Rob't
Anderson, Jn'o   Brown, Jn'o
Arnold, Jonath'n   Brisco, Walter
Adams, Rob't   Brown, Jn'o, inmate, single
Allison, Jn'o   Brown, Cha's, d'o
Adams, Sam'l   Brown, Rich'd, d'o
Allison, Ja's, single   Baird, Jn'o, d'o
Adams, Jn'o   Brown, Tho's, d'o
Adams, Sam;l   Bratton, Cha's, d'o
Beeson, Jn'o   Cook, Jerem'h
Brownfield, Cha's   Con, Wm.
Brownfield, Tho's   Cracraft, Wm.
Brownfield, Joseph   Cornwell, Jn'o
Beeson, Jacob   Campbell, Wm.
Brown, Peter   Curry, Geo.
Boner, John   Cain, Sam'l
Boner, Wm.   Castile, Alex'r
Buskirk, Mich'l   Clark, Wm.
Baird, Rob't   Calvin, Geo.
Baird, Marg't   Cornwell, Jn'o
Baird, Jn'o   Corden, Rob't
Bigham, Hugh   Collins, Jn'o
Brown, Ja's   Collins, Jos'h
Brown, Jn'o   Curethers, Tenis
Bellenger, Geo.   Case, Wm.
Bryan, Ja's   Caller, Martin
Brownfield, Rich'd   Cable, Mich'l
Brown, Manus   Calvin, Geo.
Bow, And'w   Collins, Henry
Barns, Lewis   Craft, George
Beeson, Henry   Camp, Rubin
Buskirk, Isaac   Clark, Sam'l
Been, Jn'o   Cole, Jn'o
Baltsel, Hendrix   Crawford, Hugh
Brown, Tho's   Crawford, Alex'r
Bruner, Leonard   Crosly, Wm.
Bruner, Geo.   Carter, Benj'n
Barker, Jn'o   Collins, Jn'o
Babbet, Jos'h   Culp, Dan'l
Bushears, Othy   Campbell, Math'w
Bushears, Zach   Crum, Adam
Brown, Basil   Cribble, Jos'h
Bushears, Ignatius   Case, Theop's
Bruner, Mich'l   Cheney, Rich'd
Buckibo, Peter   Crawford, Jon'h
Burkirt, Mon. Jn'o   Cornwell, Wm.

Inhabitants of Manallen Township

Crawford, Ja's
Coleman, Nath'l
Curence, Jn'o
Craft, Benj'n
Carvin, Jesse
Coleman, Jacob
Coose, Mich'l
Colvin, Wm.
Crabill, Sam'l
Cally, Peter
Caffin, Mr., Sen'r
Copperight, Peter
Case, Joseph
Cain, Math'w
Coose, Jacob
Coose, Mich'l
Colson, Uriah
Campbell, Collin
Chambers, Jon'n
Clark, Jn'o
Colson, Jn'o, single
Collins, Ja's, d'o
Crawford, Jos., d'o
Crawford, Eph'm, d'o
Chaffin, Tho's, d'o
Calman, Leonard, d'o
Craig, James
Craft, Sam'l
Dawson, Nich'l
Dawson, Widow
Downard, Jn'o
Davidson, Wm.
Deems, Jn'o
Ditch, Cath'e
Dunlap, Rob't
Dawson, Jn'o
Dougless, Sam'l
Dinbo, Rob't
Downs, Jerem'h
Davis, Moses
Downs, Thomas
Downs, Widow
Douglass, Wm.
Deems, Lewis
Dunlap, And'w
Deeth, James
Deeth, Randolph
Davis, Tho's
Deeth, Ja's
Deeth, Edw'd
Dych, Jn'o
Downard, Ja's, single
Downard, Jacob, d'o
Downard, Tho's, d'o
Dunlap, Rob't, d'o

Douglass, Eph'm, d'o
Donoldson, Jn'o, d'o
Dawson, Henry, d'o
Dougharty, Rich'd, single
Deen, Jn'o, do.
Evans, Fran's
Ester, Jacob
Ester, Mark
Elliot, Edw'd
Elliot, Tho's, single
Finley, James
Finton, Milol, single
Falls, Rich'd
Fallimore, Jn'o
Franks, Henry
Frame, Tho's
Frame, David
Frame, James
Funt, Philip
Frazier, And'w
Finton, Mich'l, single
Frame, Tho's
Guard, Jerem'h
Galaspy, Wm.
Guest, Benj'n
Gattis, Rob't
Gattis, Tho's
Gallahar, Ja's
Garden, Geo.
Gilmore, Hugh
Gilbert, Nich's
Grub, Sam'l
Gilion, Jn'o
Gattis, Jn'o
Gilson, Jn'o
Gist, Solomon
Goodwin, Thomas
Gullick, Dan'l
Goldwin, Step'h
Giffin, Gasper
Gillion, Hugh
Gray, Wm.
Greg, Thomas
Guget, And'w
Gattis, Henry
Greer, Henry
Gibney, Jos'h
Gugil, Dan'l
Gist, Tho's, single
Goodwin, Ja's, d'o
Greer, Jn'o, d'o
Hall, Jn'o, Sen'r
Huston, Jn'o
Hanthorn, Jn'o
Harmon, Cha's

Inhabitants of Manallen Township

Hestor, Jn'o
Hog, David
Hoover, And'w, Sen'r
Hewit, Jacob
Hankins, Rich'd
Hugins, Wm.
Hankins, Rob't
How, James
Hackney, Aaron
Harlin, Geo.
Howard, Gideon
Hoover, Jacob
Hain, Wm.
Hoof, Amos
Hebes, Jacob
Huckelbery, Geo.
Harrison, Jn'o
Huffman, Jn'o
Hilleker, Geo.
Hester, Jacob
Hosteter, Nich's
Hickman, Cha's
Hughs, Wm.
Hickinbottom, Mary
Huskins, Jerem'h
Huskins, Uzeriah
Huskins, Ezeriah
Hoover, Henry
Hankins, Jn'o
Hatfield, Edw'd
Hatfield, Adam
Hoak, Peter
Howard, Tho's
Heaton, Jn'o
Hall, And'w
Hallick, Tho's
Hall, Edw'd
Hart, Henry
Hawthorn, Jn'o
Hawthorn, Ja's
Hendrix, Leonard
Hendrix, Jn'o
Harmon, Geo.
Harmon, Ja's
Hackney, Harmon
Huffman, Geo., single
Haggin, Ja's, d'o
Hall, Jn'o, d'o
Huggins, Jn'o, d'o
Huggins, Wm., d'o
Huffman, Geo., d'o
Hoover, And'w, d'o
Jolliffe, Wm.
Jackson, Ab'm
Jackson, Hugh
Myers, Jn'o
Myers, H

Johnson, Eph'm
Jones, Jn'o
Jones, Tho's
Jackson, Rob't
Jennings, David
Jackson, Henry
Jones, Jonathan
Kindle, Rubin
Kindle, Benj'n, single
Kindle, Ja's
Kidwallader, Rese
Kidwalleder, Septimus
Kidd, Jn'o, single
Kindle, Tho's
Lemon, Jn'o
Lyon, Sam'l
Little, Josh'a
Lindle, Jerem'h
Lackey, Jn'o
Linn, And'w
Landison, Levy
Little, Ananijah
Lettar, Jn'o
Little, Absalom
Laughlin, Jn'o
Little, Jn'o, single
Laughlin, Hugh
Lucas, Abr.
McCoy, James
Mooney, Jn'o
McLain, James
McLain, Sam'l
McLain, Jn'o
McLain, Alex'r
McCleland, Wm.
Martin, Jn'o
Musgrove, Sam'l
Moore, Mich'l
McCra, Rob't
Murphy, Jn'o
Murphy, Wid'w
McDowell, Jn'o
McDonold, Mary
McCullough, Ja's
Moore, Augustine
McHarry, Jn'o
Moore, Philip
McChristy, Arth'r
Morrison, Wm.
Mash, Wm.
McWilliams, Sam'l
Mills, Ja's
Martin, Jn'o
McWilliams, Jn'o
Messmore, Jn'o

Inhabitants of Manallen Township

Myers, Jn'o
Myers, Henry
McCreary, Hugh
Millar, Ludwic
Millar, David
Millar, Jonath'n
Meetson, Jn'o
Maffet, Jn'o
Myers, Widow
Mears, Wm.
McCarty, Jn'o
McCarty, Sam'l
Maffet, Adam
Meynor, Wm.
McClelon, Widow
McDowell, Wm.
McDowell, Arth'r
Millar, Sam'l
Moore, Astin
McKimm, Wm.
McKinley, Sam'l
McCarty, David
McCarty, Nath'l
Moore, Geo.
McDonald, Jn'o
McFadyen, Jn'o
Mynor, Jacob
McClean, Cha's
McFarlain, Wm.
McCoy, Rob't
Muster, James
McGowan, Sam., single
McCleland, Alex'r, d'o
Murphy, Jacob, d'o
McCleland, Hugh, d'o
McCarty, Ad'm, d'o
Millar, Nich's, d'o
Millar, David, d'o
Moss, Wm., d'o
McFadyen, Ja's, d'o
Nelson, Jn'o
Newkirk, Tunis
Napp, Jacob
Napp, Peter, single
Neilly, Tho's
Osburn, Jona'n
Olton, Mary
Overturf, Felty
Olepham, And'w
Olton, Jn'o, single
Orison, Jn'o, d'o
Patton, Jn'o
Pisor, Henry
Phillips, Isaac
Pearce, Geo.

Pearce, Isaac
Porter, Jn'o
Patrick, Peter
Porter, Nath'n
Pollock, Jn'o
Purdum, Jn'o
Philips, Jn'o
Patrick, Jn'o
Parr, Sam'l
Pounds, Sam'l
Pettigem, Wm.
Porter, Armstrong
Parks, Ezekiel
Parks, Jn'o
Price, Jos'h
Pratt, Jn'o
Pratt, Jerem'h
Powers, Jn'o
Pattix, Jona'n
Porter, Jos'h
Palmer, Jn'o
Parish, Wm., single
Parson, Jn'o, d'o
Porter, Wm., d'o
Parker, Geo.
Porter, Cha's
Reed, And'w
Rowland, Jon'a
Reese, Sam'l
Richy, Jn'o
Rabb, And'w, Esq.
Rabb, Sam'l
Reeves, Sam'l
Rumley, Jerem.
Reador, David
Reador, Jacob
Rail, Wm.
Rail, Tho's
Rankin, Ja's
Rankin, Wm.
Rope, Wm.
Raley, Jn'o
Ridick, Wm.
Ross, Jos'h
Rail, Noble
Riggs, Sam'l
Roberts, Roger
Rude, Ashur
Rutter, Benj'n
Rutter, James
Rude, Zely
Rankin, Hugh, single
Rumley, Henry, 'do
Robbot, Bricent
Sutton, Isaac

Inhabitants of Manallen Township

Sutton, Sam'l
Sutton, Moses
Smiley, Wm.
Shuter, Philip
Springer, Josiah
Stevens, Charles
Sacket, Sam'l
Shaham, Wm.
Springer, Nath'n
Stevens, Augustine
Swan, Hugh
Sutton, Isaac
Sprout, Sam'l
Shelby, Josh'a
Springhill, Mich'l
Suck, David
Snider, Jn'o
Sills, Rudy
Springer, Dennis
Sutton, Isaac, Jun'r
Springer, Levy
Sturgeon, Rob't
Stitt, Jn'o
Sebb, Anth'y
Steel, Ja's
Scoley, Wm.
Scott, Tho's
Salady, Philip
Salady, Jn'o
Salady, Jacob
Shahan, Tho's
Sern, Fred'k
Swingler, Henry
Smith, Rob't
Smith, Geo.
Sterret, Tho's, single
Stokely, Jn'o, d'o
Sacrets, Wm., d'o
Sacket, Aaron, d'o
Steward, Jn'o, d'o
Smith, Wm., d'o
Sterret, Isaac, d'o
Sprout, Jos'h, single
Sterret, Isaac, d'o
Sutton, Amelek'h
Troutman, Geo.
Todd, Jn'o
Tabot, Patrick
Todd, Jn'o
Tatman, Joseph
Truman, Tho's
Tatman, Jn'o
Tomson, Ja's
Tanner, Rich'd
Todd, Edw'd

Tait, Jn'o
Thomson, Tho's
Ungan, Ragan
Urana, Leonard
Uach, James
Urana, Martin
Upp, Jacob
Walter, Conrad
Waits, Jos'h
Work, Sam'l
Williams, Cha's
Warford, Wm.
White, Sam'l
Wilson, Alex'r
Wilson, Tho's
Wilson, Henry
Wilson, David
Watson, Jn'o
Warner, Jn'o
Walter, Rich'd
Watt, Rich'd
Williams, Ja's
Winters, Ja's
West, Jn'o
Winget, Caleb
Walters, Jacob
Walters, Henry
Wood, Edw'd
Watson, Jn'o, single
Watson, Geo., d'o
Walters, Jac'b, d'o
Wilson, Sam'l, d'o
Wilson, Henry, d'o
White, James, d'o
Work, Henry, d'o

INDEX

ABRAM Enoch 40
ADAIR William 1
ADAMS Alexander 31
  Andrew 56
  James 10
  John 60
  John 31
  Robert 60
  Samuel 60
AGNEW Isaac 16
  James 16
AKER Simon 49
ALBEN William 1
ALEXANDER Adam 1
  Hugh 27
  Mary 10
  Nathaniel 49
  Samuel 31
ALLEN Benja'n 1
  David 1, 10
  Hugh 60
  James 10
  John 10
  William 1
ALLEOT Robert 31
ALLIMONG Nich'w 26
ALLIS Jn'o 20
  Mark 20
ALLISON ----- 20
  Andrew 20
  James 60
  John 60
  Moses 49, 59
ALTMAN ----- 56
  Anthony 27
  Gasper 27
  Peter 26
  William 26
AMBERSON John 31
  William 23
AMELONG Christopher 49
AMMON George 27
ANDERSON ----- 20
  David 20
  Isaac 57
  James 40
  John 60
  William 1, 31, 49, 56, 57
ANDREWS Francis 31
  William 1
APPLEGATE Benjamin 1
  Daniel 1
  Samuel 1
  William 1

ARCHER Anth'y 40
  John 40
  Joseph 1
  William 40
ARCHIBALD Benjamin 10
ARCHIBOLD Patrick 59
ARDROY John 31
ARMSTRONG Benjamin 56
  John 31
  Thomas 1
  William 31
  William B. 31
ARNOLD Andrew 10
  Daniel 49
  John 49
  Jonath'n 60
ARRAT Christian 26
  John 27
ARROWSMITH James 40
ASHCRAFT Amos 40
  Ephraim 40
  Ichabud 40
  John 40
AVERLY Leonard 40
  Nicholas 40

BABBET Jos'h 60
BACCHUS Cath'e 40
  Peter 40
  William 40
BACKUS Philip 10
BAGGS Andrew 32
  John 31
  Mathew 32
  William 32
BAGLE Elias 40
BAILEY John 56
BAILY Silas 40
BAIRD Charles 20
  George 31
  James 20
  John 49, 60
  Margaret 60
  Moses 20
  Robert 60
  William 31
BAKER Andrew 1
  Nicholas 40
  Philip 41
BALES Jesse 41
BALTSEL Hendrix 60
BARIHILL Alexander 20
BARKELY James 40
BARKER James 11
  John 10, 60

  Jos'h 10
  Joseph 10
  William 10
BARKLEY Elijah 10
  John 1, 40, 41
  Joseph 2
BARNHART Jacob 27
  William 27
BARNS Ezekiel 40
  Lewis 60
  Robert 1
  Silvanus 40
  William 27
BARNY Andrew 49
BARR Alexander 20
  James 20, 32
  John 23, 58
  Mary 20
  Robert 49
  Samuel 32
BARRACKHAMER John 1
BARRACKMAN Frederick 40
  George 1
  John 41
  Michael 1
  Peter 1
BARRAT Samuel 41
BARTLETT Thomas 11
BASH Martin 49
BATTAN Jos'h 41
  Thomas 41
BATTERSHELL Freeman 11
  John 11
BAUL Richard 10
BAUM Chris'n 27
BAXTER Samuel 1
BAYS David 49
  Hugh 49
  William 49
BAZEL Mathew 1, 2
BEACON William 32
BEAKEM John 32
BEALER Christopher 16
BEALL Robert 17
BEALOR Jos'h 32, 49
BEAR Adam 49
  Henry 49
  John 20
  Rudolph 49
  Rudy 49
BEARS Frederick 20
BEASY John 32
BEATY Jos'h 23, 32
BEATY Samuel 27
  William 27, 32

INDEX

BECK Jeremiah 41
BECKET John 1
  Joseph 1, 10
  Mary 1
  Robert 32
BEDSWORTH Joseph 1
BEEN John 60
BEER James 32
  John 32, 57
BEESON Henry 60
  Jacob 60
  John 60
BELL Agness 32
  Hump'y 40, 41
  James 40, 41
  John 17, 41
  Jos'h 17
  Robert 49
  Samuel 17
  Thomas 23
  William 27, 49
BELLENGER George 60
  Rudy 40
BENNET Benjamin 26
BENSON James 32
BENTLY Mary 20
BERGER Frederick 1
BERLIN Jacob 32
BERRY John 11, 17
  Joseph 40
  Samuel 40
  Thomas 41
BEST Robert 27
  Thomas 11
  William 27
BEVELIN John 40
BIARLY Jacob 32
  Michael 32
BIGGART John 2
  Samuel 1
BIGHAM Hugh 60
BISHOP William 23
BLACK James 40, 49
BLACKBURN Anth'y 32
  John 32
  Jos'h 31, 32
BLACKE Thomas 10
BLACKSTON James 32
BLAIR John 32
BLAKE Nicholas 40
BLAKELEY Robert 1
BLAKLY William 17
BLANE Ephraim 49
  Widow 20

BOALL Charles 31
  Henry 32
  James 32
BOGEL --- 20
BOGGS James 23
BOLE James 49
BONER John 60
  Mathew 1
  William 60
BONNETT Lewis 40
BOURNS James 17
BOVAIRD James 27
BOVEL John 1
BOW Andrew 60
BOWERS Abraham 59
  Basil 40
  Robert 17
  Thomas 40
BOWIN Samuel 41
BOWMAN Jacob 1
  Philip 40
BOYARS Andrew 10
  Samuel 10
BOYD Darcus 27
  John 16, 20
  John W. 32
  Nathaniel 1
  Samuel 32
  Thomas 32, 49
  Widow 1
BOYERS Andrew 11
  James 10
  John 11
  Philip 41
  Samuel 10
BOYLS William 40
BOYS James 10, 11
  Richard 11
BRACKEN William 57
BRACKINRIDGE Hugh 23
BRADFORD Charles 10
  Widow 10
BRADIBURY Coonrad 40
BRADLEY John 49
  Moses 10
  Samuel 49
BRADLY John 23
BRADY William 23
BRAND James 11
  John 10, 59, 60
BRANKER Henry 49
BRANNON George 31
  John 27
  Peter 23
  William 27

BRANT Barney 1
  Edward 2
BRATTON Charles 60
BREWER Benjamin 16
  Mary 32
  Peter 32
  Samuel 17
BRIDGWATERS Samuel 40
BRIGGS John 1
BRINEY John 49
BRINY Peter 27
BRISBY William 27
BRISCO Walter 60
BRODDY Hugh 1
  William 1
BRODSWORD Mathias 32
  Peter 32
BROOKS Aaron 20
  Jeremiah 41
BROWN --- 20, 27, 56
  Andrew 58
  Basil 40, 60
  Benjamin 1, 31
  Charles 60
  Eliezer 10
  James 49, 58, 60
  John 27, 32, 60
  Josh 40
  Manus 60
  Nathan 10
  Peter 60
  Richard 60
  Robert 32, 41
  Steven 41
  Thomas 60
  William 10, 17, 20, 27,
    49, 56
BROWNFIELD Charles 60
  James 56
  Joseph 60
  Richard 60
  Thomas 60
BROWNLEE Hugh 27
BROWNLOW James 1
  Thomas 1
BRUMFIELD Emson 40
  James 49
  Robert 40
BRUNER George 60
  Leonard 60
  Michael 60
BRYAN James 60
  William 49
BRYNEY Adam 32
BRYSON James 27

INDEX

BUCHANNAN William 32
BUCHANNON Alexander 40
  David 32
BUCK John 32, 59
BUCKIBO Peter 60
BUDD Joseph 1
  Joshua 1
BUHAR Christian 23
BULLOCK --- 58
BUNTS Locwic 59
BURCH John 1
BURCHAM Benijah 1
BURCKHAM Catharine 40
BURD Thomas 57, 58
BURGAN Daniel 1
BURGES Richard 1
BURGESS Ann 1
BURGH Robert 60
BURK John 40
BURKART Jacob 23
BURKIRT Mon. John 60
BURNS Arthur 1
  James 20, 32
  Patrick 10
  Samuel 1, 10
BURROWS James 23
BURT Ebenezer 11
  Jotham 11
BUSH Daniel 27
BUSHEARS Ignatius 60
  Othy 60
  Zach 60
BUSKIRK Isaac 60
  Michael 60
BUTLER Edward 17
  Rachel 41
  Thomas 49
BYARS Andrew 32
  Coonrod 49
  George 27
  Philip 59
BYERS Philip 40
BYRAM Edward 32

CABLE Michael 60
CAFFIN Mr. 61
CAHILL Edward 20
CAIN Mathew 61
  Samuel 60
CAINS Daniel 42
CAINT Absalom 17
CALDWELL Alexander 33
  Elberton 41
  Isaac 17
  John 20

  Josiah 33, 41
  Mathew 33
  Robert 2, 21, 33
  William 21, 33
CALGAN Patrick 27
CALHOON Adley 2
  James 57
  Thomas 2
CALKLAZER Abraham 33
  David 33
  John 33
CALLAHAN William 41
CALLAN Patrick 50
  William 27
CALLER Martin 60
CALLY Peter 61
CALMAN Leonard 61
CALVIN George 60
  James 41
  William 2
CALWELL Andrew 33
CAMARA Adam 27
  John 27
  Ludwick 27
CAMBLE James 56
CAMERON Gilbert 23
CAMP Garrard 33
  Joseph 2
  Mathias 33
  Rubin 60
CAMPBELL --- 21
  Charles 49, 56
  Collin 61
  George 49
  Henry 2
  James 11, 17, 20, 21, 33, 41, 56
  John 21, 23, 33, 50
  Josiah 50
  Mathew 60
  Michael 33
  Patrick 33
  Robert 23
  Thomas 56, 57
  William 21, 60
CANE Martha 50
CANNON Daniel 11
CAPLE Jacob 27
CARMICAL Daniel 2, 58
  John 2, 11, 23
CARNAHAN David 27
  James 33
  John 33
CARR Elijah 41
  Elisha 41

  James 11, 21
  John 41
  Moses 41
  Thomas 41
CARROL James 27
CARROLL James 20
  Taylor 2
  Thomas 23
CARSON Alexander 11
  John 11
  Richard 33
  William 11
CARTER Barziila 49
  Benjamin 60
  Precilla 59
CARUTHERS James 33
CARVER Jacob 49
CARVIN Jesse 61
CASADY Daniel 33
CASE Butler 2
  Joseph 61
  Meshach 2
  Theop's 60
  William 60
CASSELMAN Henry 2
  Jacob 23
  John 2
  William 2
CASTILE Alexander 60
CASWELL Samuel 50
CATHCART David 11
CATT George 41
  John 41
  Michael 42
  Philip 41
CAVENAUGH John 17
CAVETT John 2
CHAFFIN Thomas 61
CHAIN --- 56
  Hugh 11
  John 17
  William 17
CHALFANTS Chads 11
CHAMBERLAIN Thomas 2
CHAMBERS Edward 2
  James 23, 33
  John 2
  Jonathan 61
  Moses 50, 56
  Thomas 23
CHAPMAN Nicholas 20
CHENEY Richard 60
  William 2
CHERRY John 11
  Peter 27

INDEX

Ralph 49
CHIPELY William 11
CHRISTY John 17, 27
  Michael 42
CHURCHILL Richard 41
CLARE Thomas 41
CLARK Benjamin 2
  George 2, 21
  James 21, 49, 50
  Jeremiah 41
  John 23, 32, 61
  Josiah 50
  Nathaniel 2
  Richard 17
  Samuel 2, 60
  William 50, 60
CLASKY Robert 21
CLAUSON Garrard 41
CLEGHORN John 21
  Mathew 21
CLEMMONS John 2
  Samuel 2
CLEMONS Ferguson 2
  Josiah 11
CLIFFORD Charles 17, 58
  George 17
  Robert 17
CLINE Jacob 50
CLINGLESMITH Andrew 27
  Daniel 27
  Jacob 50
  John 27
  Peter 27
  Philip 27
CLIPENER George 50
CLOVER Jacob 41
COCHRAN Andrew 32
  John 32
  Robert 50
  William 21
COCKEYOWENS John 2
COE Benjamin 33
  Ebenezer 33
  James 33
COFMAN Michael 58
COLE John 60
COLEMAN Jacob 61
  Nathaniel 61
  Nicholas 57
COLEMER Coonrod 50
COLLINS Henry 60
  James 61
  John 23, 41, 60
  Josiah 60
COLMAN Christopher 41

COLSON John 61
  Uriah 61
COLVIN William 61
COMBS Jesse 41
  Jonathan 41
  Joseph 11, 41
  Josiah 41
CON William 60
CONKLE John 27
  Michael 27
CONN George 41
CONNELL Ann 17
  Zachariah 17
CONNERS Samuel 11
CONRAD John 33
CONSLY Peter 50
CONWAY Hugh 27
COOK Catharine 27
  Edward 2
  Jeremiah 60
COON Anthony 41
  Coonrad 41
  Joseph 41
COOPER James 57
  John 32, 41
  Samuel 27, 33
  William 27, 33, 42
COOSE Jacob 61
  Michael 61
COPPER Charles 17
  Josiah 17
COPPERIGHT Peter 61
COPSTICK Samuel 2
CORDEN Robert 60
CORK Benjamin 11
CORNWALL Widow 17
CORNwELL John 60
  William 60
CORT Joseph 2
CORTNEY William 21
COULTER Ely 32
  Samuel 50
COURTNEY Eliz'a 50
COUZ Craft 33
COUZE Philip 50
COWAN Mathias 32
COWEN Daniel 33
  Patrick 33
COX John 41, 56
  Joseph 41
COYL Manasah 17
CRABILL Samuel 61
CRACRAFT William 60
CRAFT Benjamin 61
  George 60

Samuel 61
CRAIG Alexander 2, 50
  James 61
  Jean 21
  John 2, 20, 50
  Samuel 21
  Thomas 23
CRAIGHEAD Robert 2
CRANMORE Agnes 23
CRAWFORD Alexander 11, 60
  Ephraim 61
  George 2, 50
  Hugh 60
  James 11, 50, 61
  John 11, 50
  Jon'h 60
  Joseph 61
  Robert 50
  Widow 11
CREANOR Philip 32
CRIBBLE Josiah 60
CRIPS John 27, 56
CRISTY James 33
  John 32, 33
CRISTY William 23
CROGHAN George 23
CROOKSHANKS Andrew 27
CROSLEY David 11
CROSLY William 60
CROSS William 41
CROUSHOUR Nicholas 41
CROW James 50
  John 20, 50
CROZIER William 21
CRUM Adam 60
CRUTCHLOW William 32
CUE James 2
CULBERSON John 27
CULBERTSON --- 20
CULP Daniel 60
CUMMINS David 57
  John 11, 58
CUMMONS John 33
CUNNINGHAM Bar'd 17
  Henry 32
  John 17
  Margaret 17
  William 2, 23
CUPPAGE Isaac 2
CURENCE John 61
CURETHERS Tenis 60
CURRY Aeneas 17
  George 60
  Myrack 17
  Robert 11

INDEX

Thomas 17
William 21, 56
CUSHMAN Isaac 41

DAGLEY Michael 12
DAILEY John 57
DALL James 42
DARR Michael 2
DAVIDS Thomas 17
DAVIDSON William 2, 61
DAVIS Azariah 3
  Benjamin 3, 11
  Hanover 28
  Hugh 23
  James 12
  John 11, 33, 42
  Mary 24
  Moses 61
  Owen 42
  Philip 42
  Samuel 42
  Thomas 11, 61
  William 33, 42, 56
  Zachariah 11
DAVISON John 33
DAVY Josiah 42
  Thomas 42
DAWSON Benoni 11
  Henry 61
  John 11, 61
  Nich'l 61
  Thomas 11, 42
  Widow 61
  William 11
DEAL William 23
DEAN Benjamin 42
  Richard 42
DECKER Jacob 2
DEDMAN Henry 50
DEDOR Jacob 28
DEEMS John 61
  Lewis 61
DEEN John 61
DEETH Edward 61
  James 61
  Randolph 61
DEHAVEN Isaac 2
DEMUS Peter 17
DENNISON Arthur 21
  John 21, 50
DEVALL Margaret 42
  Notley 42
  Pierce 42
DEVALT Macklin 57

DEVORE Moses 3
  Samuel 3
DEVOSS Joseph 33
DIBLE Jacob 33
DICKESON Joshua 11
DICKSON Joseph 12
  Josiah 21
  Silas 12
  Stafford 12
DIER John 33
DILFORTH Widow 50
DILL Francis 33
DILLENGER Barbary 42
DILWORTH Benjamin 50
  John 50
DINBO Robert 61
DITCH Catharine 61
DIVIS Elias 50
DIXON George 56
  Joseph 56
  Samuel 56
  Silas 2
DONAHE John 21
DONAHOO John 50, 56
  William 50
DONALDSON Susanah 42
DONOLD --- 21
  James 21
  Moses 21
DONOLDSON Hugh 23
DONOLDSON Isaac 21
  John 17, 61
DORSON John 11
DOUGHARTY --- 3
  James 42
  John 11
  Martha 23
  Richard 61
DOUGLASS Andrew 24
  Ephraim 24, 61
  William 61
DOUGLESS Samuel 61
DOUSMAN John 3, 24
DOWDEN Nathaniel 11
DOWNARD Jacob 61
  James 61
  John 61
  Thomas 61
DOWNEY John 56
  William 3
DOWNING John 50
  William 50
DOWNS Jeremiah 61
  Thomas 61
  Widow 61

DRAGGO Baltzar 42
  Peter 42
DRAGO William 42
DRAIN Francis 33
DRAKE John 42
DRENNON John 2
DRENON Thomas 3
  William 2
DRUM Philip 2
  Simon 27
DUFF Alexander 3
  John 3
  Oliver 3
DUFFEY Michael 42
DUGAN Robert 11
DUKE Charles 23
DUMBAL Abraham 59
  Peter 59
  Philip 59
DUMMIT William 17
DUNBAR John 23
DUNCAN David 23
  James 33
DUNFIELD Frederick 23
DUNGAN John 2
  Joseph 2
  Nathan 2
DUNKAN James 28
DUNLAP Adam 11
  Andrew 61
  John 11
  Robert 61
  Samuel 12
  William 11, 21
DUNN Hugh 17
  Nehem'h 17
  Thomas 11
  William 2
DUNNING Robert 23
DUNSETH James 50
DUSH George 42
DYAL Edward 17
DYCH John 61
DYE John 3

EAGER John 50
  Josiah 50
  William 50
EAKER George 59
EAKIN Benjamin 33
  James 50
EARL Robert 3
EATON James 21
ECKLES Charles 33
  William 21

INDEX

EDWARDS Peter 42
EKIN Alexander 3
  James 3
  Robert 3
  William 50
ELDER David 50
  Joshua 56
  Robert 57
ELLIOT Edward 61
  John 3
  Thomas 50, 61
  William 24
ELROD Tedor 3
ELSWORTH Andrew 28
EMLEY John 3
ENGLISH James 21, 33
ERWIN Joseph 17
  Samuel 21
ESPY Jacob 50
  William 17, 57
ESSECK William 58
ESTALL Daniel 12
  Thomas 12
ESTER Jacob 61
ESTER Mark 61
EVALT Samuel 24
  Samuel 26
EVANS Edward 3
  Francis 61
  Henry 17
  Hugh 42
  Jacob 17
  Samuel 57
  Widow 56
  William 24
EVERER Adam 28
EVERET Jacob 28
EVERLY Adam 42
EWING John 57

FACIT Thomas 42
FAILS Alexander 56
FALLIMORE John 61
FALLS Richard 61
FANSIER William 42
FARGUSON James 50
  Widow 56
FARIES James 28
FARRAN Hugh 33
  John 57
FAST Francis 42
  Jacob 42
  Nicholas 42
FEALS Alexander 21

FELL Benjamin 3
  John 3
FERNSLY James 24
FERREE John 24
FERRY Hugh 42
  James 42
  Widow 24
FERST Jacob 42
FINK Daniel 42
  Henry 42
FINLEY Andrew 33
  David 3
  Isaac 42
  James 3, 28, 61
  John 3
  Josiah 24
  Michael 34
  Richard 42
  Samuel 12, 57, 58
  William 50
FINNEY James 3
  William 3
FINTON Michael 61
  Milol 61
FISHER Abel 59
  Adam 50
FISKIS Abraham 50
  Charles 50
  Garard 50
  John 50
FITCH John 3
FITZGERALD Barth'w 33
FLECK James 58
  John 3
  Robert 58
  William 42
FLEEHARTY James 42
FLEMING Nathaniel 12
FLEMING Robert 28
FLEMMING James 24
  John 3, 21, 57
  Lewis 17
  Robert 17
  Thomas 17
FLETCHER Thomas 34, 50
FLINN William 24
FLOWERS Lombard 42
FLUD Michael 12
FLYNN William 17
FOCKLER Adam 3
FOREMAN Charles 28
FORKNER Alexander 12
  David 12
FORSTER James 34

FORSYTHE Robert 3
  Thomas 17
  William 3
FOSTER Agnus 42
  Benjamin 3
  Jeremiah 12
FOWLER Alexander 24
FRAIZE William 42
FRAME David 61
  Jacob 50
  James 61
  Thomas 61
FRANCE Henry 50
FRANCIS Philip 24
FRANKS Henry 61
  Jacob 42
  Michael 42
FRAZIER Andrew 61
  Rory 24
FREEMAN Adam 28
  Philip 58
  Samuel 12
  Thomas 12, 28
  William 24, 28
FREETLY Jacob 28
  Martani 28
FRICK George 34
  Henry 34
  Nicholas 34
FRIRKNEY Henry 42
FRITCHMAN Adam 28
FROST James 3
FRY Michael 33
FRYAR Robert 3
FULLERTON Humphrey 57, 58
FULTON Abraham 34, 57
  Henry 34
  James 21, 33, 34
  John 12, 28, 33
  Robert 34
  Samuel 3
  William 33
FUNK Martain 34
FUNT Philip 61
FURSER George 17
FUTHY Samuel 12

GABON John 34
GAFF James 51
GALASPY William 61
GALBRAITH Thomas 58
GALBREATH John 51
  Robert 24
GALLAHAR Barney 21
  James 21, 61

INDEX

GALLAHER Emanuel 28
GALLASPY George 43
GAMBLE William 12
GAMMELL Samuel 12
GARDEN George 61
GARDNER Archibald 3
  William 3
GARNER Abraham 17
  Edward 18
GARR Gasper 3
GARRAT John 12
GARRISON Leonard 43
GARVIN Josiah 51
  Marvin 34
GASTON Alexander 3
  John 4
  William 4
GATHER William 43
GATTIS Henry 61
  John 61
  Robert 61
  Thomas 61
GAUT Mathew 18
GEORGE Adam 28
GIBB Hugh 4
  Robert 57
GIBBONS James 43
GIBNEY Josiah 61
GIBSON Edward 12
  John 12, 24, 56
  Levy 34, 56
  Samuel 12
  Thomas 24, 56
  William 12
GIFFIN Gasper 61
  John 51
GIFFY Thomas 34
GILBERT Nicholas 61
GILION John 61
GILKEY David 43
  William 34, 42
GILL Hugh 34
GILLILON Henry 12
GILLION Hugh 61
GILMORE David 4
  George 12
  Hugh 61
  James 43
  John 4
  Mathew 43
  William 4
GILSON John 61
GIRTS Harmon 21
  Henry 21

GIRTY John 24
  Thomas 24
GIST Solomon 61
  Thomas 61
GLASGOW John 43
  Samuel 18
GLASS John 24
  Robert 3
GLEN James 21
GLENN James 51
  John 34
  William 4
GLOVER Uriah 43
GOE John 3
  William 3
GOLDEN John 12
GOLDWIN Stephen 61
GOODWIN Benjamin 43
  James 61
  Josiah 43
  Thomas 61
GOOSMAN Christopher 43
GORBY Thomas 3
GORCHAM John 12
  Thomas 12
GORDAN John 34
GORDEN James 56
GORDON Archibald 4
  James 51
  Robert 34
GORELY John 51
GOST Craft 17
GOUDY John 3
GRAHAM David 18
  John 43
  Noble 17
  Richard 17
  William 51
GRAMES Peter 24
GRATZ Barnard 4
GRAY James 34, 42
  Jeremiah 42
  Robert 4
  William 61
GREEN Lavor 12
  Tamor 3
GREER Henry 61
  Isaac 4
  James 3
  John 4, 61
  Lawrence 3
  William 51
GREG Thomas 61
GRIER Thomas 12
GRIFFIN Charles 43, 58

GRIFFITH John 43
GRIMES Donold 24
GRINSTAFF Lewis 43
GRIST William 3
GROSS Christian 28
GROUS Peter 28
GROUSHOUR John 28
GRUB Samuel 61
GRUBB Jacob 24
GUARD Jeremiah 61
GUEST Benjamin 61
GUFFY Henry 24
  James 24, 34
GUGET Andrew 61
GUGIL Daniel 61
GULLICK Daniel 61
GUNN William 24
GUTHRIE Alexander 21
  James 51
  John 51
  William 21, 51
GUTHRY John 51
GUY James 51, 58

HABBAGE Andrew 34
HACKNEY Aaron 62
  Harmon 62
HAGAN John 57
HAGARTY Nicholas 24
HAGGIN James 62
HAGGIS Samuel 34
HAIN William 62
HALFERTY Edward 58
HALL --- 58
  Andrew 62
  Edward 62
  Henry 4
  James 21
  John 4, 34, 61, 62
  Joseph 4, 13
  Robert 28, 34
  Stephen 4
  William 4
HALLICK Thomas 62
HALLIN Thomas 43
HALSCLAY James 43
HAM Coonrod 34
HAMILTON Archibald 24
  James 4, 34
  John 24, 43
  Robert 34
HAMLEE John 58
HAMMOND Daniel 4
  James 4
  Samuel 4

INDEX

HAMSON William 28
HAND Levy 44
HANDLEY Samuel 34
HANDLYN John 24
HANKINS John 62
  Richard 62
  Robert 62
HANNA Eliz'h 43
  John 58
  Margaret 12
  Robert 28, 43, 58
  William 12
HANNON John 12
HANTHORN John 61
HAPPY James 18
HARBRIDGE Edward 21
HARDESTY Thomas 12
HARDIN Abraham 43
  Benjamin 43
  Charles 56
  Eden 43
  John 43, 44
  Mark 43
  Martin 43
  Mary 43
  Robert 43
  Steven 43
  Thomas 44
HARDISTY Francis 12
HARE Michael 51
HARKIM Peter 12
HARLAIN James 12
HARLIN George 62
HARMAN Peter 28
HARMON Charles 61
  George 62
  James 62
HAROLD Christopher 28
  John 28
HAROLD Peter 28
HARPER James 12
  Robert 34
  Robert 57
  Thomas 34
HARRA Charles 4
HARRING Coonrad 51
HARRIS Benjamin 4
  Jonathan 44
HARRISON Benjamin 13
  Charles 12
  John 62
  Nicholas 12
  Robert 43
  Widow 12

HART Elizah 4
  Henry 62
  John 56
HARTLEY Robert 51
HARTMAN Henry 58
HASELEY Henry 28
HASLEP James 18
  Robert 34
HATFIELD Adam 18, 62
  Edward 62
HAUTT Peter 43
HAWFIELD Catharine 43
  Devalt 43
  Mathias 43
  Peter 43
HAWK Coonrad 28
  Henry 58
HAWTHORN James 62
  John 62
  Widow 12
HAY Michael 59
HAYMAKER Jacob 24
HAYS Andrew 12
  Christopher 34
  John 28
HEADEN Christopher 4
HEADY Thomas 43
HEATON John 43, 62
HEBES Jacob 62
HELDIBRANT Philip 4
HENDERSON John 34
  Rev'd Mr. 58
HENDRIX Abraham 34, 43, 58
  Absalam/Absalom 12, 58
  Daniel 12, 58
  John 62
  Leonard 62
  Simon 44
HENRY Aaron 12
  Frederick 28
  George 51
  John 34, 57
  Robert 21
HERINGTON Barth'w 51
HERSHA Peter 4
HESTER Jacob 62
HESTOR John 62
HETH Henry 24
HEWIT Jacob 62
HICKINBOTTOM Mary 62
HICKMAN Charles 62
  Eliz'a 18
  Francis 18

  Tram'l 18
HICKS Samuel 18
HILANDS Barney 28
  Widow 56
HILL --- 28
  David 34
  Frederick 34
  Gasper 34
  John 43
  Joseph 4
  Peter 28, 34
  Robert 43
  Stephen 4
  William 12, 43, 56
HILLEKER George 62
HINDMAN Robert Peter 34
HISE Henry 58
HITE Sarah 18
HOAK Andrew 28
  Peter 62
  Samuel 28
HODGE John 18
HOG David 62
HOGAN Gaian 34
  John 34
HOGELIN William 43
HOGG Michael 4
HOLLIS William 34
HOLLOBACK George 43
HOLMES Jonathan 24
  Samuel 4
HOOF Amos 62
HOOK Henry 59
HOOVER Andrew 62
  Henry 2
  Jacob 62
  Peter 4
HOPKINS John 51
  Josiah 51
  Josiah 57
HOPLETS Michael 34
HOSTETER Nicholas 62
HOUSER John 28
HOUSMAN Christopher 4
  John 4
HOUT Eliz'a 43
HOW James 62
HOWARD Charles 43
  Gideon 62
  James 44
  Philip 12
  Thomas 62
  William 56
HOWEL Andrew 4
  Luellen 4

INDEX

Philip 4
HUBER George 59
HUCKELBERY George 62
HUCKLEBERRY Frederick 43
HUDD John 12
HUDSKINS Samuel 4
HUDSON John 43
HUEY Thomas 18
  William 34
HUFFMAN George 62
  Henry 34
  John 62
HUFFNAGLE Mical 24
  Michael 28, 58
HUFHANS Josiah 59
HUFNAGLE Michael 57
HUGGINS John 62
  William 62
HUGHES John 4
HUGHEY James 43
  Robert 12
HUGHS James 57
  John 28
  William 21, 62
HUGINS William 62
HULL Solomon 12
HUME John 43
HUMES John 4
HUNTER Cyrus 18
  James 51
  John 51
  Patrick 34
  Robert 28, 34
  William 34
HURST Henry 51
  Nathaniel 51
  William 51
HUSKINS Ezeriah 62
  Jeremiah 62
  Uzeriah 62
HUSTON James 56
  John 12, 61
  Margaret 18
  Robert 43
  William 18
HUTABAUGH George 21, 28, 56
HUTCHISON George 59
  James 34, 57
  John 51, 56, 57
  Rebecca 18
HUTTEN Mary 4
HYNES Alexander 4

ICEMAN Peter 28

INGLE John 4
INMAN Henry 51
  William 51
IRELAND Hans 28
  John 13
IRWIN Agnes 24
  Alexander 28
  David 24
  Henry 34
  John 13, 24, 28, 35
  Joseph 13
  Laurence 28

JACK John 35, 51
  Mathew 28
  Patrick 51
  William 28
JACKSON Abraham 62
  Henry 62
  Hugh 62
  John 28
  Robert 35, 62
  Samuel 13
  Thomas 35
JACOBS Benjamin 57
JAMISON John 51
  Mathew 4
  Robert 4, 51
  Widow 58
  William 58
JARVIS Richard 51
JEANES Widow 56
JEFFRIES John 57
JEMMISON Francis 51
  Marmaduke 51
JENNINGS David 62
JINKINS John 44
  Philip 44
  William 44, 51
JOHN David 44
  John 13
  Latta 52
  Thomas 44
JOHNSON Andrew 4
  Benjamin 24
  Ephraim 62
  Henry 18
  James 4, 18, 35
  Jonathan 4
  Peter 4
  Richard 4
  Roger 18
  Thomas 35
JOHNSTON Alexander 35, 58

Archibald 13
  Charles 51
  Hugh 35
  James 35, 51
  John 24, 35
  Richard 35
  Samuel 13
JOICE William 21
JOLLIFFE William 62
JOLLY David 35
  Nelson 44
  Thomas 21
JONES Amos 59
  Edward 4
  Evan 35
  Isaac 59
  Jacob 5
  John 62
  Jonathan 62
  Joseph 4
  Morgan 44
  Philip 18
  Thomas 4, 35, 51, 62
  William 4
JOURDAN Edward 13
JUMP John 18

KAPLE Jacob 29
KARR Martha 24
  William 29
KAYS Robert 51
KEASY James 24
KEELING John 13
  Patrick 13
KEFFER Henry 35
KELLER Peter 5
KELLS George 59
KELLY Edward 21, 57
  James 5, 56
  John 5, 57
  Mathew 35
  Patrick 44
  Samuel 44
  Thomas 35, 44
KEMSON John 35
KENNEDY Hugh 5
  Robert 5
  William 5
KENNISON James 44
  Josiah 44
KENT Thomas 5
KEPLEY Christopher 5
KEPPLE Nicholas 29
KER James 35

INDEX

KERN Mathias 59
  William 59
KERNS John 5
KERR George 35
  James 35
  Joseph 5
  Paul 35
  Robert 5, 35, 51
  William 5, 35
KERROLL Anthony 44
  Joseph 5
KESLER Peter 18
KETCHEM Stephen 5
  William 5
KIDD Daniel 44
  John 62
KIDWALLADER Rese 62
  Septimus 62
KIFER Henry 29
KILE Samuel 56
KILFILLEN Thomas 35
KILGORE David 51, 58
  John 5, 51
  Patrick 35
KILLBRIGHT James 35
  Daniel 21
  Samuel 21
KILPATRICK Samuel 57
  William 58
KIMBLE Jacob 29
KINDLE Benjamin 62
KINDLE James 62
  Rubin 62
  Thomas 62
KING James 29
  William 44
KINKEAD Andrew 51
  James 24, 35
  Samuel 44
KIRK James 29
  Vincent 5
KIRKPATRICK Alexander 35
  George 35
  James 28
  John 35
  Joseph 35
  Thomas 35
  William 51
KISTOR Ludwick 29
KITHCART James 35
KITSOR Philip 29
KNOX David 35
  John 13
  Robert 58
KOLFMAN Michael 59

KOONTZ Philip 28
KROFFORD Robert 59
KYLE Edward 35
  John 5, 35
KYSER Benjamin 24

LACKEY John 62
LAMBERT John 22
LANDERS John 5
LANDISON Levy 62
LANE Isaac 24
LANEY Daniel 58
LANOM William 44
LANTERMAN Peter 5
LAPPIN William 5
LARRIMOR David 29
LARRIMORE Samuel 5
LARSH Charles 44
  Paul 44
LASLEY John 22, 57
LASWELL Thomas 44
LATIMORE George 35
  John 36
LATTA Ephraim 21
  Moses 51
  William 35
LATTIMORE George 5
  William 52
LAUGHEAD Joseph 35
LAUGHLIN Hugh 62
  James 13
  John 62
  Peter 13
  Reynolds 56, 57
  Robert 13
LAVERE Daniel 58
LAVOUR Barnard 35
  Barth'w 52
  Christian 51
  Henry 52
LAWRANCE Philip 44
LAWSON John 13
  Thomas 13
LAZIER Abraham 51
  Daniel 52
  John 52
LAZURE George 22
  Hiat 24
LEECH James 35
  Samuel 35
LEMON Archibald 56
  Henry 5
  James 56
  John 62
  Joseph 5

  Thomas 5
  William 57
LEONARD James 21
LERUE Abraham 5
LESLY John 44
  Thomas 44
  William 44
LETTAR John 62
LEVINGSTON John 44
LEVY Isaac 18
LEWIS Evans 13
  Ezekiel 35
  Francis 13
  Jacob 13
  Philip 44
  Samuel 51, 52
LICH Francis 13
LIDICK Jacob 52
  John 52, 56
LIGHT Jack 35
  John 35
  Peter 35
LIGHTENBERGER George 24
LINCH John 13
  Patrick 13
LINDLE Jeremiah 62
LINDOR Simon 44
LINDSEY David 18
  Edm'd 18
  Hezekiah 35
  John 35
  William 5
LINEHART Christian 24
LINN Andrew 5, 62
  John 5
  Samuel 18
LINSEY Anthony 13
  Jolson, Jn'o 13
LITSLONE Abraham 29
LITTLE Absalom 62
  Ananijah 62
  Jacob 51
  John 62
  Joshua 62
  Samuel 5
LITTLETON John 5
LOCHRY Jeremiah 52
  Mary 51
  William 52
LOCK Benjamin 5
LOGAN David 35
  John 5
  Patrick 13
  Thomas 35
  William 13

INDEX

LONG Benjamin 5
  John 35
  Ludwick 29
  Nicholas 29
  Thomas 5
  Tobias 29
  William 35
LOSSET Stophel 59
LOUDON Thomas 18
LOURY John 18
LOUTZINHISER Jacob 35
  Peter 35
LOVE William 21, 29
LOVENGUIRE Christopher 51
LOWERS Robert 21, 52, 56
LOWREY William 56
LOWRY James 5
  John 5
  Stephen 5
LUCAS Abraham 62
LUKIS John 44
  Richard 44
  Robison 44
LUTE Nicholas 58, 59
LUTES George 36
  Philip 36
LYNCH George 13
  James 13
  John 44
  Samuel 13
LYNN Andrew 13
  James 13
  Patrick 13
LYON John 13, 44
  Samuel 62
  William 29

MACKEY William 6
MACKLIN Jacob 57
MAFFET Adam 63
  John 63
MAGNOR Redman 6
MAHARGE Peter 58
MAIN George 45
  Henry 45
  John 45
  Philip 45
MAINS Robert 37
MALSON Daniel 36
  Nicholas 36
MANN John 37
  Joseph 22
  Thomas 37
  William 37
MAPPINS James 6

MARCHANT David 29
  Frederick 29
MARSHALL Archibald 52
  Henry 59
  Hugh 45
  James 52, 53, 57
  John 57
  Ralph 45
  Robert 52
  William 36, 53
MARTAIN Asa 44
  John 44, 45
  Thomas 18
  William 36
MARTIN George Adam 6
  Hugh 52
  James 36, 37
  John 18, 59, 62
  Joshua 6
  William 25, 36
MASH William 62
MASON Isaac 18
  John 18, 19, 45
  Joseph 18
  Martain 45
  Philip 18, 45
  Thomas 29, 36
MASSEY John 19
  William 18
MASTERSON Hugh 13
  Sarah 44
MASTIN Peter 6
MATHEWS Ezekiel 22, 57
  John 18, 57
MATHIAS Daniel 29
  George 29
MATTHEW James 6
MAXWELL Adam 22, 53
  James 6
  John 6, 13
  William 14, 52, 53
McANULTY Josiah 36
  Richard 36
McBRIDE James 52
  John 36
  Thomas 24
  William 36
McBRIER Nathaniel 29
McCALL Barn's 52
McCANN Henry 36
  John 36
McCARTNEY George 53
  Peter 25
McCARTY Adam 63
  David 63

  John 63
  Nathaniel 63
  Robert 7
  Samuel 63
McCASKY --- 59
  Mathew 37
McCASLIN James 36
McCAW David 36
  John 36
McCHRISTY Arthur 62
McCIBBIN John 52
McCLAIN Daniel 14
McCLANAHAN John 52
McCLANAN Thomas 56
McCLANNAHAN James 52
McCLARY Thomas 37
McCLEAN Alexander 22
  Charles 63
  James 22
McCLELAND Alexander 53, 63
  George 52
  Hugh 63
  James 45, 53
  John 36, 52, 56
  William 62
McCLELLAN William 45
McCLELLAND James 25
  John 13
McCLELON Widow 63
McCLENEHAN Thomas 52
McCLINTIC Alexander 19
  Henry 36
  Samuel 36
McCLOUD Murdock 25
McCLURE George 5
  James 6
  John 52
  Samuel 36
McCOLISTER Alexander 22
  James 22
McCOLLISTER John 14
McCOLLOUGH Samuel 57
McCOMB James 37
McCONNELL Adam 6
  John 6, 36
  Robert 7
  William 29
McCORD James 36
McCORMACK James 14
  William 14
McCOWAN Alexander 13
  John 14
  Josiah 13

INDEX

McCOY Daniel 58
  James 62
  Robert 63
  Samuel 7
  Thomas 52, 56
McCRA Robert 62
  William 14
McCRACKEN John 52
McCRACKIN John 58
McCRADY John 22, 56
McCREA Thomas 57
  Widow 57
McCREARY Andrew 45
  Hugh 63
McCULLOUGH Andrew 36
  David 18
  James 62
McCUNE Andrew 6
  Thomas 6
  William 57
McCURDY James 36, 37, 58
McDADE Hugh 36
McDONALD John 25
McDONOLD Alexander 45
  Da'd 45
  Daniel 25
  George 52
  Hugh 25
  Isaac 45
  John 36, 45, 52, 63
  Mary 62
  Patrick 25
McDOWEL Edward 59
  Robert 58, 59
McDOWELL Arthur 63
  John 62
  William 60, 63
McEDOO John 45
McELROY Widow 25
McELROY William 6
McELWANE Francis 25
McFADYEN James 63
  John 63
McFARLAIN John 44
  Walter 52
  William 53, 63
McFARLIN James 56
McFARSON Alexander 44
McGARRAUGH Joseph 6
McGAUGHAN Mark 5
McGEARY Rachel 52
  William 52
McGINNIS Charles 25
  Francis 52
  Thomas 6

McGOLDIRCK James 25
McGOMERY John 57
McGOWAN Samuel 63
McGREGOR Collins 29
McGREW Alexander 36
  James 37
  John 36
  Simon 37
  William 37
McGRUDER Hezekiah 5
McGRURY Thomas 36
McGUGIN Alexander 52
McGUIRE Charles 57
McGWIRE John 29
  Patrick 14
  William 53
McHAFATY Adam 45
  John 18
  William 45
McHAFFATY Alexander 44
McHAFFY Moses 13
  Samuel 13
McHARRY John 62
McHENRY Josiah 37
  Kain 37
  Malcam 36
McHUTCHIN Alexander 36
McHUTCHIN James 36
McINTERFER Daniel 29
McINTIRE --- 22
  Andrew 22
  Elenor 45
  John 5, 18, 45
  Thomas 13
  William 5, 57
McKAY Mary 24
McKEE Alexander 56
  David 29, 37
  Hugh 29
  James 29, 52
  John 25, 37, 52
  Margaret 29
  Robert 29
  William 5, 18, 56
McKENNY Isaac 52
McKIMM William 63
McKINLEY David 18
  Robert 25
  Samuel 63
McKINNEY Henry 6
  Mathew 6
McKINNY Alexander 52
  Hugh 52
  John 37
McKINTS William 59

McKISSICK Daniel 57
  Isaac 52
McKNIGHT Thomas 6
  William 52
McLAIN Abijah 6
  Alexander 62
  James 56, 57, 62
  John 14, 59, 62
  Laughlin 25
  Paul 53
  Robert 6, 45
  Samuel 62
McLAUGHLIN Edward 6
  Henry 6
  John 14
  Robert 14
  Samuel 6
  Thomas 44
  William 36
McLEAN Joseph 6
McLUCAS John 37
McMAHON John 57
McMANUS Widow 58
McMASTERS James 52
  William 52
McMEANS Robert 6
McMICAL Samuel 36
McMILLEN John 58
McMULIN Samuel 58
McMULLEN Han'h 29
  James 14, 44
  John 14, 36
  Robert 52
  Samuel 14
McMULLIN James 45
  John 58
McNAB George 13
McNAUGHER Hugh 37
McNEAL Arthur 14
  John 6
  William 56
McPIKE Daniel 45
McQUESTON James 53
McQUILKIN James 53
McRIGHT William 6
McRILAND John 53
McWHISTER William 52
McWILLIAMS John 62
  Samuel 62
MEANS John 18
MEANT Mathew 14
MEARS William 63
MEASURE Thomas 13
MECKLIN Devalt 29
  Jacob 29

INDEX

Michael 29
MEEK John 53
MEEKS Jacob 18
MEETSON John 63
MELLENDOR David 36
  John 36
  William 36
MELLON Hugh 37
MERCIAL Gasper 37
MERRIFIELD Mary 44
  Richard 44
  Samuel 44
MESOR Abraham 45
MESSMORE John 62
MESSOR Hugh 18
MEYNOR William 63
MILBURN David 6
MILES Thomas 25, 58
MILLAR Christian 29
  David 63
  Eliz'a 25
  Gideon 37
  Isaac 36
  James 29, 37
  John 36, 59
  Jonathan 63
  Ludwic 63
  Mathew 29
  Michael 36
  Nicholas 63
  Robert 22, 57
  Samuel 63
  Silas 36
  William 26
MILLEGAN --- 26
  James 18
  William 52
MILLEGEN James 25
  John 37
MILLER Isaac 37
  John 25
  William 13
MILLIRONS Jacob 29
  Philip 29
MILLS Edward 5
  James 62
MINOCHRE John 58
MINOR John 18
MINSOR Daniel 45
MINTOR John 18
MIRE Adam 29
  Christian 29
MITCHEL Alexander 6
  Samuel 6

MITCHELL Andrew 52
  Charles 36
  Ebenezer 6
  Edward 6
  Hannah 6
  Hugh 36
  James 14, 53
  John 6, 57
  Joseph 6, 57
  Mathew 6
  Nathaniel 44
  Robert 6
  William 6, 13, 22, 44
MOLLAN William 14
MOLVIN William 59
MONTGOMERY Hugh 6
  James 59
MONYSMITH Christopher 29
MOODY James 13
MOONEY James 6
  John 62
MOOR Hugh 29
  James 29
  John 29, 56
  William 29
MOORE Aaron 44
  Ann 45
  Astin 63
  Augustine 62
  Daniel 59
  Ezekiel 45
  Forgy 6
  George 52, 63
  James 6
  John 37, 52
  Michael 62
  Philip 62
  Robert 6, 45
  Samuel 45
  Thomas 14, 45
  William 6, 36, 56
MOOREHEAD Thomas 6
MOORHEAD Samuel 56, 58
MORE Thomas 13
MORECRAFT John 18
MOREHEAD Alexander 5, 57
  Joseph 5
  Samuel 36
MORELAN Josiah 14
MORELAND Jason 5
MORELIN Richard 5
  William 13

MORGAN David 44
  George 18
  Morgan 5
  William 6
MORHEAD Forgy 56
MORLAND Alexander 13
  David 13
  William 14
MORRIS Isaac 14
MORRISON Daniel 52
  John 18
  Mathew 52
  William 62
MORROW Samuel 36
MORTON John 36
  Thomas 6
  William 6
MOSS William 63
MOUNT William 56
MOUNTS Provid'e 18
  Providence 18
MUFFLEY John 29
MULLEN James 5, 37
MURPHEY William 45
MURPHY Hugh 7
  Jacob 63
  John 36, 53, 62
  Patrick 18, 25
  Robert 13
  Samuel 18
  Widow 62
  William 13
MURRY Neal 52
  Thomas 45
MUSAN John 36
  Philip 37
MUSE Fantley 6
MUSGROVE Samuel 62
MUSTER James 63
MYARS Adam 29
MYER Eliz'a 45
MYERS Adam 45
  Eliezer 24
  Frederick 45
  Henry 63
  James 24
  John 63
  Widow 63
MYNOR Jacob 63

NAGLE Frederick 58
NALDER John 29
NAMAN Harmon 37
  William 37

INDEX

NAPP Jacob 63
  Peter 63
NASH Thomas 7
NAUGLE Andrew 25
NEAL John 37, 53
  Robert 25
  Widow 14
  William 53
NEEL James 45
  Josiah 45
NEELEY Mathew 14
NEELY Joseph 37
NEESBIT John 7, 19
  Nathaniel 19
  Samuel 19
NEGLEY Alexander 25, 58
NEILLY Benjamin 29
  Hugh 53, 57
  Thomas 63
NELLSON Agness 29
  William 29
NELSON John 63
  Joseph 14
NESBIT Jerem'b 37
  William 37
NESLEY Adam 59
NEWEL Samuel 7
NEWELL Hugh 37
  James 53
  John 53
  Joshua 53
  Margaret 37
  Robert 37, 53
  William 37
NEWKIRK Tunis 63
NEWLING Paul 37
NEWMAN Isaac 45
NEWN Christopher 45
NICHOLAS James 14
  Thomas 37
NICHOLASON Josiah 25
NICHOLS John 37, 53
  Robert 53
  William 53
NIGH Jacob 7
NIPLEY Mary 7
NITTERFIELD William 7
NIXON Jonathan 45
NOBLE Richard 14
NORNIVAL John 7
NORRIS Joseph 14
  William 14
NOTTS Solomon 45

O'FINN John 14

O'HARA Hugh 25
O'HARRA Arthur 53
  James 25
O'KAIN Patrick 37
O'NAIL Charles 30
OAKERMAN Stophel 53
OCULL James 45
OGDEN David 7
OLDHAM Isaac 7
OLEPHAM Andrew 63
OLIVER Andrew 30
OLREY Henry 59
  Henry 60
OLTON John 63
  Mary 63
ORISON John 63
ORMSBY John 25
ORR George 60
  Robert 30
  William 14
OSBURN John 37
  Jonathan 63
  Samuel 37
  William 37
OTTERMAN Ludwick 30
OURY Adam 30
  Christopher 29
OVERLY Bastion 59
  Martin 59
OVERTURF Felty 63
OWEN Widow 14
OWENS Thomas 7
  William 37
OWINS William 25

PAIN Samuel 45
PAINTER George 30
  Jacob 30
  John 30
PALMER Adam 53
  John 58
  John 63
PANE Jonathan 46
PARCHMENT Nicholas 25
  Peter 25
PARISH Edward 14
  Richard 14
  William 63
PARKER George 63
  Robert 14
  Samuel 46
PARKILL David 19
PARKS David 14
  Ezekiel 63
  Hugh 30

  John 63
  Samuel 15
PARR Isaac 22
  James 22
  Samuel 22, 63
PARRIS William 15
PARSON John 63
PARTMISER Adam 53
PATERSON John 45
PATRICK John 22, 63
  Peter 63
PATTERSON Francis 37
  James 7, 14, 37
  John 7, 15, 37
  Peter 7
  Robert 7
  Samuel 22
  Thomas 7, 14
  William 15
PATTIX Jonathan 63
PATTON Francis 46
  John 63
  Joseph 7
  Robert 46
  Thomas 53, 56
  William 22
PATTY George 30
PAUL Jacob 7
  James 37
PEARCE George 63
  Isaac 63
PECK William 30
PENDERGRASS Garrard 37
PENNY Joseph 14
PEOPLES James 37
  John 53
  Samuel 53
PERKINS Eliezer 59
PERKY Christopher 15
PERRY David 19
  James 7
  John 30
  Samuel 37
  William 22, 30
PERSHON Christian 53
  Frederick 53
PERSON John 45
PETERS Godfrey 45
  John 58
PETERSON --- 22
PETTIGEM William 63
PETTIT Elias 22
  Jeremiah 7
PETTYJON John 45
PHILIP Thomas 46

INDEX

PHILIPS John 45, 63
  Jonathan 15
  Mary 46
  Richard 14
  Samuel 14
  Theop's 45
PHILLIPS Isaac 63
  Thomas 25
PHIPS John 14
PIERCE Andrew 7
  Charles 7
  Elisha 14
  Isaac 19
  James 7
  John 7
  Joseph 7, 14
  Lewis 7
  Philip 46
PIERCEHOUR George 46
PILES Zachareus 46
PIPER James 19
  William 58
PISOR Henry 63
PITTS William 7
PITTSOR Christopher 46
POCK Michael 46
  Nicholas 46
POINTS Nathaniel 7
POLLAN Samuel 14
POLLOCK James 25, 53, 58
  John 63
  William 14
POMROY John 22
POPE William 14
POREKINS Eleazar 60
PORRINGER Samuel 46
PORTER Armstrong 63
  Charles 63
  David 37
  Hugh 58
  John 19, 63
  Josiah 63
  Nathaniel 63
  Robert 19
  William 63
POTTER Samuel 30
POUGH Jacob 46
POUNDS Samuel 63
POUNDSTONE Richard 46
POURSLY David 14
POWELL James 14, 25
  Richard 46
  Thomas 45
  William 25
POWER Benjamin 14

POWERS Abraham 53
  Eli 14
  Jacob 53
  James 7, 14, 53
  John 63
PRATHER Bas'l 45
  Thomas 14
PRATT Jeremiah 63
  John 63
PRESSOR Henry 7
PRICE Christopher 14
  Josiah 63
  Thomas 30
PRICKER Adam 30
PRICKET Josiah 46
PRIGHBLIL Peter 46
PRIGHTBILL Jacob 46
PRITCHARD Richard 7
PROCTOR John 53
  William 53
PROVINCE Sarah 45
PURDER John 59
PURDUM John 63
PURDY John 14
  Robert 7
PUSEY Henry 37

QUIGLEY Cary 53
  Hugh 25
QUILLEN Ambrose 7
QUIN John 53
QUISENBURY Moses 15
  William 15
QUORDIN Adam 46

RABB Andrew 47, 63
  Samuel 63
RAGAN Garard 19
  Philip 38
  Resen 15
RAIL Noble 63
  Thomas 63
  William 63
RALEY John 63
RALPH Thomas 38
RALSTON John 53
  Joseph 8
  Robert 54
  William 38
RAMAGE John 25
RAMMAGE William 7, 25
RAMSEY --- 22, 56
  James 38, 56, 57, 58
  Thomas 46
  William 15

RANEY Lawrence 38
RANKIN David 54, 57
  Hugh 63
  James 15, 63
  Samuel 15
  Solomon 25
  William 7, 63
RARDON John 8
RATTAN John 7
RAY Henry 19
  Josiah 53
RAYBURN Robert 19
RAYNOR Stophel 54
REA James 38
READ Robert 38
  William 57
READOR David 63
  Jacob 63
REARDON Dennis 38
  John 38
REAS Jonathan 46
REASOR Frederick 54
REED Andrew 63
  Caleb 46
  James 8, 25, 38
  John 7, 15, 58, 59
  Richard 46
  Robert 58
  Thomas 46
  William 15
REEL Gasper 25
REESE Samuel 63
REEVES Abner 7
  Samuel 63
REILEIGH Charles 54
RESNOR Peter 7
RETHERFORD John 38
REYBURN Adam 38
REYNOLDS James 57
  John 22
  Josiah 53
  William 38
RHAY Richard 15
RHODES Anthony 46
  Henry 19
RHOI Samuel 15
RICE Edm'd 19
  Frederick 30
RICH Jacob 46
RICHARDS Charles 26
RICHARDSON orphans 58
RICHEY John 15
  Mathew 15
  Samuel 15
RICHIE Robert 46

INDEX

RICHY Edward 38
  John 63
RICKET Philip 15
RIDDICK John 30
  William 25
RIDDIN William 25
RIDDLE John 53
  William 30
RIDICK William 63
RIFLE George 46
  Jacob 46
  Mathias 46
  Nicholas 46
RIGGS Nathaniel 15
  Samuel 63
RIGHT Henry 46
  John 19
RINEHART Andrew 25
RINN Nicholas 30
RITCHEY William 7
RITCHY Abraham 7
  William 7
ROBB Isaac 7
  Nicholas 7
ROBBOT Bricent 63
ROBERTS Phil. 46
  Roger 63
  Thomas 56
ROBERTSON Alexander 15
  Henry 46
  James 15, 38, 46
  John 15, 38, 53
  Margaret 53
  Samuel 53
  Susan'h 46
  Thomas 38
  William 15, 53
ROBINS Daniel 46
  Isaac 46
  Obdeiah 8
  Richard 46
  William 47
ROBINSON Andrew 26, 54
  Hugh 54
  James 25, 38
  Robert 54
  William 53, 54
ROBISON Alexander 7
  Andrew 8, 58
  David 8
  John 59
  William 56
RODEARMOR John 25
ROGERS Andrew 7
  George 19

Hannah 46
Henry 46
John 15, 46
Jolly 56
Jonathan 47
Joseph 15
Philip 46
Robert 38, 57
Thomas 15
Tully 46
ROGRALD James 53
ROISTILL Andrew 30
ROLETER Peter 25
ROLLINS Anthony 38
  Henry 38
  James 38
RONEY Patrick 38
ROPE William 63
RORER Frederick 56, 57
ROSS John 38, 46
  Josiah 63
  Robert 15
  Samuel 38
  Tasf 15
  Thomas 25
  William 15
ROUNT Jacob 22
ROUP Francis 30
ROW Jacob 46
ROWE George 58
ROWLAND Evan 46
  Jonathan 63
ROWLEY John 53
ROZE Enoch 19
RUBBILL Samuel 46
RUDDIN William 25
RUDE Ashur 63
  Zely 63
RUDIBAUGH Adam 38
  Christopher 19
RUFINDER Simon 54
RUGH Anthony 54
  Catharine 30
  Jacob 30
  Michael 30
  Peter 30
RULLE Samuel 38
  Thomas 38
RUMLEY Henry 63
  Jeremiah 63
RUSSEL David 56
RUSSELL James 22, 54
  John 22, 46
  Thomas 46
RUTHERFORD John 56

RUTTER Benjamin 63
  James 63
  John 46
RYAN George 54
  Jacob 25
  James 25
  John 7
  Michael 7
RYBOLT Jacob 25
RYNAMAN Christopher 25
RYNN John 30
RYNOR Stophel 56
RYSOR Daniel 25

SACKET Aaron 64
  Samuel 64
SACRETS William 64
SALADY Jacob 64
  John 64
  Philip 64
SALSBERRY William 47
SAMBEL Michael 56
SAMPLE David 38
  Ezekiel 39
  Samuel 26
SAMPSON John 8
  Thomas 9
  William 8
SAMS Adam 38
SANDERSON Henry 38
SANDS James 8
SANKSTON Isaac 47
SARREN Samuel 22
SCANTLIN John 15
SCATTOB Henry 59
SCOLEY William 64
SCOTT --- 22
  Hugh 56
  James 9, 22, 54
  John 8, 39, 47
  Josiah 54, 56
  Knight 54
  Samuel 9
  Thomas 64
  William 15, 38
SEARS Daniel 47
SEBB Anthony 64
SECRETS Valentine 19
SEES Christopher 54
SEGORINE Josiah 59
SELDERS George 54
SELFACE John 30
SENF Gasper 59
SERN Frederick 64

INDEX

SEWARD James 15
 Samuel 15
SEYNOR Michael 54
SHAFER Adam 30
SHAHAM William 64
SHAHAN Thomas 64
SHAKLETT Benjamin 47
 John 47
SHALTZBERGER Henry 54
SHANKLIN George 15
SHANKS John 47
SHANNON Henry 39
 John 38
 Richard 59
 Samuel 59
SHAROW Jacob 59
SHARP Andrew 58
SHAVER Jacob 8
 John 8
 Paul 8
 William 8
SHAW James 38
 William 30
SHEAK Christian 30
SHEANOR Jacob 30
 Mathias 26
SHEARER David 54
 John 16
SHEEK Lodwic 59
SHELAH Michael 9
SHELBY David 47
 Joshua 64
SHELHAMER Peter 30
SHEPARD John 54
SHEPHARD Henry 8
SHEPHERD Edward 26
 John 54
SHEPPARD Solomon 8
SHERER Timothy 38
SHERRY Barny 38
SHETLER Peter Coonrod 38
SHIELDS David 39, 57
 George 8
 John 30
 Samuel 39
 William 39
SHIGLEY Peter 59
SHILLIN George 38
SHINS George 47
SHIPLER Mathias 8
 Peter 8
 Philip 8
SHIRE Nicholas 30
SHIVELY Christopher 47
 John 47

Philip 47
SHOEMAKER John 47
SHOLEY Adam 47
SHORES Richard 15
SHOTTS Michael 30
SHRADER Aaron 54
 Jacob 30
 William 54
SHRIEVES Samuel 15
SHRUM John 30
SHUTER Philip 64
SHUTTLEWORTH Thomas 47
SIERS David 47
SILKWOOD Basil 47
SILL George 8
 William 8
SILLS Rudy 64
SILSOR George 47
 John 47
 Jonathan 47
SIMMERMAN Michael 26
SIMONS --- 26
 Josiah 26
SIMPSON Allen 47
 Gater 47
 Gilbert 15
 James 54, 56
 Joseph 8
 Mathew 54
 Thomas 30, 54, 56
 Widow 56, 57
SIMRAL James 57
SINNET Jacob 8
SKINNER --- 22
SLOAN David 54
 John 22, 54
 Samuel 22, 54, 57
 William 54
SMALLMAN --- 26
 Thomas 26
SMART Joseph 15
SMILEY John 19
 William 47, 64
SMIRL George 22
SMITH --- 22
 Amos 47
 Andrew 16, 39
 Augustus 47
 Corbet 15
 David 19
 Deverux 26
 Doctor 26
 George 30, 38, 64
 George William 39
 Henry 47

James 39
John 38, 48, 56, 57, 58
Michael 19, 30
Moses 19
Peter 47
Philip 30, 47, 54
Philly 47
Rev'd Mr. 56
Robert 3, 22, 54, 64
Samuel 30, 58
Shrist'r 30
Thomas 54
William 8, 15, 19, 47, 56, 57, 64
William Corbet 15
SMITLEY Gasper 54
 Gasper 54
 Nicholas 54
SNAIR Michael 48
SNIDER John 64
 Peter 39, 58
 Rudolph 47
SNODGRASS Charles 47
 Samuel 19
SORRELS James 56
 Samuel 54
SOXMAN Christian 22
SPARKS Benjamin 9
 Isaac 16
 Richard 9
 Walter 9
 William 16
SPARR George 30
SPEARS Jacob 8
SPEELMAN John 54
SPEERS Rogana 8
SPRINGER Dennis 64
 John 8
 Josiah 64
 Levy 64
 Michael 8
 Nathaniel 64
 Zedick 47
SPRINGHILL Michael 64
SPROUT Josiah 64
 Samuel 64
ST. CLAIR General 8, 26, 54, 58
STANDIFORD Ephraim 8
STARET Joseph 8
STATIA Peter 19
 Thomas 19
STEEL Adam 16
 James 8, 47, 64
 Joseph 8

81

INDEX

William 8
STEER Barnard 54
  Jacob 54
STERLING James 47
STERRET Isaac 64
  James 8
  Thomas 64
STEVENS Amos 58
  Augustine 64
  Benjamin 15
  Charles 64
  Daniel 15
  Henry 47
  Isaac 9
  John 8
  Joseph 16
  Levy 8
  Richard 15
  Samuel 16
  Thomas 8
STEVENSON Edward 47
  James 19, 22
  Jean 22
  John 19
  Marcus 19
  Thomas 22
  William 22, 54
STEWARD Andrew 22
  Archibald 30
  David 19
  George 47
  James 8, 19
  John 8, 19, 54, 64
  Robert 19
  Thomas 8
  William 15, 19, 38, 54, 56
STEWART Andrew 56
STILL James 54
  William 16
STILLWELL Ann 47
  Josiah 47, 48
  Obdeiah 47
STILTS Anthony 15
  John 47
STIMBLE Isaac 38
STINSON James 9
STITT John 64
STIVERS Rubin 8
STOCKBERGER Mathias 54
  Michael 22, 54
STOKELEY Thomas 30
STOKELY John 64
  Nch'h 38
STOOLFIRE Christopher 8

STOTT Adam 30
STOUK Philip 47
STRAIN Michael 26
  Samuel 16
STRAW Jacob 30
STREADLER John 47
STREAKER Elias 38
STUART James 39
  John 16
STUDIBERGER Abraham 38
  Josiah 38
  Peter 19, 38
  Philip 38
STUDWILL Charles 15
STULL William 15
STUOT Adam 38
STURGEON Robert 64
  Samuel 38
STUTSTILL John 54
SUCK David 64
SUMMERVILLE Alexander 38
  Francis 15
  John 9
SUNDERLIN John 8
SUTHERDAY Jacob 47
SUTHERFIELD Benjamin 47
SUTTON Amelek'h 64
  Benjamin 59
  David 8
  George 58
  Isaac 63, 64
  James 47
  Moses 64
  Samuel 64
  Thomas 58
SWAB George 38
SWAN George 38
  Hugh 64
SWARDS Samuel 8
SWEADWINK John 47
SWEAK George 15
SWEANK Jacob 15
SWEANY Thomas 8
SWEARINGEN John 47
  Van 8, 9, 47
SWIFT John 38
SWINGLER Henry 64
SWITZAR Peter 47
SWOOP Nicholas 39
SYPE Adam 30
SYPHRED Jacob 8
SYPHRITZ Bostion 54
  Joseph 8

TABOT Patrick 64
TAIT John 64
  Samuel 39
TAITT David 58
TANNER George 30
  James 55
  Philip 9
  Richard 64
  William 22
TANNIHILL Adam'n 26
TARR John 39
TARRANCE Hugh 16
  James 19
  Joseph 16
  Samuel 16
TARRENGER Michael 39
TATMAN John 64
  Joseph 64
TAYLOR Abraham 39
  George 9
  Henry 9
  Isaac 9
  John 39, 55, 58
  Robert 22, 31
  Thomas 22
  William 16, 55, 57
TEAGARDEN Daniel 9
TEAMOR Adam 55
TEBALT George 48
TEMPLETON James 48
TERRET Charles 26
TETRICK John 16
THOM John 55
THOMAS Aeneas 48
  Edward 48
  Garrard 30
  Henry 48
  John 48
  Josiah 48
  Owen 48
  William 30
THOMPSON Anthony 22, 39
  Cornel's 9
  Daniel 9
  General 26
  Henry 19
  James 9, 16, 22, 26, 39, 56
  John 9, 22, 26, 39
  Josiah 55
  Moses 9
  Nathan 16
  Robert 19
  Samuel 39
  Widow 57

INDEX

William 55
THOMSON Thomas 39, 64
THORN John 55
  Joseph 9
  Robert 9
THREW Adam 39
TINNEL William 22
TITTLE Peter 55
TIVEBAUGH Coonrad 48
TOBIN George 48
TODD Edward 64
  John 64
  Samuel 39, 55, 56
  William 55
TOMLING Zedic 55
TOMSON James 64
TOPPINS Robert 55
TRAVIS John 16
TRENT --- 26
TREUX Obdeiah 48
TRIMBLE Archibald 55
  George 56
  James 19
  John 55
  Thomas 55
TROOP Widow 26
TROUTMAN George 64
TRUBY Catharine 30
TRUMAN Thomas 64
TUCKER George 48
  John 48
  Samuel 48
TULLY Aaron 9
TURNER John 30
TUSH Catharine 48

UACH James 64
UNGAN Ragan 64
UPP Jacob 64
URANA Leonard 64
  Martin 64

VALENTINE William 26
VANCE David 39
  George 39
  Margaret 19
  Robert 55
  William 9, 39
VANDEREN John 19
VANDIKE William 31
VANDOLAN Peter 9
VANKIRK Jacob 16
VANLEER Mathew 39
VANMETER Jacob 9
  John 9

VANTRESE Isaac 9
VEAL John 39
VERNON John 19
VIGAL Philip 39
  William 39
VORAS Ralph 23
VOUCHER Peter 9

WADDLE Daniel 10
  James 10, 55
  John 10
  Peter 9
  Robert 55
  Samuel 23, 31, 56
  William 55
WADE Alexander 48
  John 48, 55
  Mary 48
WADMAN Christopher 48
WAGNOR tory 55
WAID George 48
  John 48
  Thomas 48
  William 48
  Windman 48
WAITS John 48
  Josiah 64
  Richard 48
WALKER Alexander 55
  Andrew 56
  Ebenezer 9
  Gedior 40
  Henry 20
  James 9, 31, 48
  John 10, 48
  Robert 9
  William 9
WALL James 10
  Walter 10
WALLACE James 39
  Richard 57
WALLING Thomas 10
WALLIS George 26
  James 23
  Richard 23
  Thomas 39
  William 16
WALSH James 31
  John 31
WALTENBAUGH Rineh'd 31
  Tedor 31
WALTER Anthony 31
  Conrad 64
  Jacob 55
  Philip 31

  Richard 64
WALTERS Coonrad 48
  Ephraim 48
  Henry 64
  Jacob 64
  John 19
WALTHOUR Christopher 39
  George 39
  Michael 39
WALTINGBAUGH Tedor 55
WARAM James 19
  John 19
WARD --- 26
  Edward 26
  John 16
WARDIN Samuel 39
WARFORD William 64
WARMAN Joseph 9
WARNACK Edward 39
WARNER John 64
  Joseph 10
WARNOCK William 9
WARREN Thomas 9
WASHINGTON his Excll'y 16
  John 16
WATERSON James 31
WATKINS Evan 48
WATSON George 64
  James 26
  John 64
  Robert 16
  Widow 55
  William 23, 39, 48, 57
WATT Richard 64
WAUGH John 31
  Paul 20
WAUSON Charles 39
  James 39
WEAGLE Isaac 31
WEAGLEY Abraham 39
WEAGLY Abraham 31
WEASNER John 55
WEAVER Adam 55
  Gasper 55
  John 31
WEBB John 48
WELKER Michael 31
WELLS Abraham 48
  Am. 48
  Benjamin 20
  James 39
  John 16, 56
  Levy 48
  Tunis 16
WELSH Charles Thomas 16

INDEX

WENSELL Philip 31
WESBY James 31
WEST John 64
WESTBAY Henry 9
WETHERINGTON Mark 48
  William 48
WETHINGTON Mary 48
WHALEY James 20
WHITAKER John 9
WHITE Agnes 39
  Andrew 9, 55
  Archibald 55
  David 55
  Henry 20
  Isaac 20
  James 48, 55, 64
  John 20, 26, 55
  Moses 20
  Patrick 55
  Samuel 64
  William 20
WHITEHEAD Val'e 39
WHITELEY Charles 48
WHITESELL Barbara 26
WHITESIDE Joseph 19
  Josiah 58
WHITESIDES Samuel 19, 55
  William 19
WHITGAR Abraham 26
WHITSEL Jacob 26
WICKERHAM Adam 9
WIGGAIN John 39
WILEY --- 56
  John 31, 55
  Mathew 16
WILFORD John 55
WILKEY James 16
  Thomas 23
WILKINS James 56
  Thomas 56
WILKINSON John 48
WILLIAMS Basil 48
  Charles 64
  Daniel 31, 39
  David 10
  Elisha 48
  George 48
  James 10, 64
  John 26
  Richard 60
  Thomas 31
  William 48
WILLIS Robert 16
WILLS Andrew 23
  James 23

WILLSON James 31
  Robert 39, 57
  Samuel 9
  William 31
WILSON Aaron 10
  Adam 10
  Alexander 64
  Andrew 19
  Benjamin 19
  Charles 31
  Col's 26
  David 16, 64
  Edward 31
  Francis 26
  Henry 64
  Hugh 9, 55, 57
  Isaac 10
  James 9, 23, 40
  John 39, 58
  Joseph 9, 57
  Josiah 23
  Robert 9
  Samuel 20, 39, 55, 64
  Thomas 9, 26, 39, 57, 64
  William 9, 16, 26
  Zachareus 10
WINEBIDDLE Conrad 26
WINEMILLER Coonrod 26
  Jacob 26
WINGET Caleb 64
WINGFIELD Henry 55
WINSELL John 31
WINSOR James 48
WINTER Thomas 55
WINTERS James 64
WINYMAKER Peter 31
WISE Jacob 26
WISEMAN John 9
WISTED Humphrey 48
WITHROW William 9
WOLF Andrew 31, 56
  Jacob 55
WOOD Daniel 48
  Edward 64
  John 39
WOODROW John 39
WOODS John 57
WOOLF Andrew 23
WOOLSEY William 10
WORK Henry 64
  Joseph 16
  Samuel 16, 64
WORKMAN William 48
WORLEY John 9

WORTHINGTON Jacob 55
  James 55
  Robert 55
  William 55
WRIGHT John 9
WRITTENHOUSE William 16
WROTHWELL Peter 9
WYRE William 40

YEAGER George 49
  Joseph 49
YEARIN George 56
YOKEY Abraham 31
YORK Ezekial 49
  Jeremiah 49
  Jesse 49
  Joshua 49
YOUGHY Christopher 55
  Peter 56
YOUNG Alexander 31, 57
  Charles 16
  Coonrod 55
  Daniel 16
  David 49
  George 16
  Isaac 16
  James 16
  Joseph 16
  Nathan 20
YOUNT Nicholas 31

www.ingramcontent.com/pod-product-compliance
Lightning Source LLC
Chambersburg PA
CBHW051658090426
42736CB00013B/2436